your guide to pensions 2006

Planning ahead to boost retirement income

By Sue Ward

Published by Age Concern England
1268 London Road
London SW16 4ER

© 2005 Age Concern England

Twelfth edition

First published 1993 as *The Pensions Handbook*

Editor Ro Lyon
Production Leonie Farmer
Design and typesetting GreenGate Publishing Services, Tonbridge, Kent
Printed in Great Britain by Bell & Bain Ltd, Glasgow

A catalogue record for this book is available from the British Library.

ISBN-10: 0-86242-409-7

ISBN-13: 978-0-86242-408-4

CONTENTS

About the author   6

Acknowledgements   7

Introduction   9

Planning ahead

How much do you need in retirement?   18

What will you have coming in?   20

How does it look?   22

Checklist of Action Points   26

State pensions

How State pensions work   38

    State Pension age   38

    Civil Partnerships and State benefits   39

    Basic Pension   41

    Additional Pension   55

    Graduated Pension   60

    Over-80s pension   61

    Pension forecasts   61

Pensions abroad   63

Pensions for widows and widowers   65

Pensions and divorce   70

Drawing your pension   72

Increasing your pension   74

Means-tested benefits for pensioners   79

Early retirement and State benefits   82

Working after State Pension age   89

Non-State pensions: the different types and frameworks

The ways in which pensions build up   92
    Defined-benefit schemes   93
    Defined-contribution (money-purchase) schemes 98

The legal frameworks   100
    Statutory schemes   102
    Trust-based occupational schemes   104
    Contract-based pension arrangements   106

Contracted in or out of S2P?   107
    Contracted-out salary-related (COSR) schemes 108
    Contracted-out money-purchase (COMP) schemes 111
    Appropriate personal pensions   113

So what sort of pension is yours?   114

The tax rules   120

Occupational pensions

How occupational schemes work   138

Should you join your employer's pension scheme?   146

Issues for women   149

Death benefits   154

Occupational pensions and divorce   158

Buying extra pension   160

Leaving an occupational scheme   168

Early retirement   181

Working after retirement age   186

How secure is your occupational pension?   189

Personal and stakeholder pensions

How personal pension schemes work   204

Stakeholder pensions   216

Buying a personal pension   220

Issues for women   229

Working after retirement age   231

Stopping paying into a personal pension   232

Increasing your pension   235

Drawing your pension   236

Further information

Glossary   252

Pension organisations   261

About Age Concern   268

Publications from Age Concern Books   269

Index   275

ABOUT THE AUTHOR

Sue Ward is a freelance journalist and researcher specialising in pensions and social security matters.

Her publications include: *Essential Guide to Pensions*, Pluto Press, 1992 (third edition); *Women and Personal Pensions* (jointly with Bryn Davies), HMSO for Equal Opportunities Commission, 1992; *Planning Your Pension: A TUC Guide*, Kogan Page, 2002; and *Changing Direction: Employment Options in Working Life*, Age Concern Books, 2002 (second edition). She is also the author of regular articles in specialist magazines such as *Pensions World and Employee Benefits*.

She was a member of the Occupational Pensions Regulatory Authority (Opra) from its setting up in 1996 until April 2002, and is a governor of the Pensions Policy Institute.

ACKNOWLEDGEMENTS

This is the latest edition of a book originally published under the title of *The Pensions Handbook*, and written by Jennie Hawthorne, in 1993. Her work on the concept, and the draft, must be fully acknowledged. With changing circumstances in the pensions world, much further work has gone into all the revisions since. I must take full responsibility for any mistakes and errors.

My thanks to Ro Lyon for her excellent editing, and to Leonie Farmer and other staff at Age Concern.

Over the years the following organisations have given generously of their time, the facts at their disposal and their opinions. All were gratefully received.

Alexander Consulting Group
The Annuity Bureau
Association of British Insurers
Barnett Waddingham (for permission to use website material about SIPPs)
Clerical Medical Investment Group Ltd
Department for Work and Pensions (Press Office)
Equal Opportunities Commission
Equitable Life
Financial Services Authority
Fiona Price and Partners
Friends Provident (for permission to use material from the leaflet *A Guide to the New Pensions Tax Regime)*
HM Revenue & Customs (formerly the Inland Revenue)
Incomes Data Services (for permission to use information from its 2003 report *Pensions After Final Salary)*

Legal and General Insurance (Ron Spill)

London Life Limited

National Association of Pension Funds

Pensions Advisory Service (TPAS)

Pensions Management Institute

Pensions Ombudsman

Pensions World

Society of Pension Consultants (for permission to use material from
The New Lifetime Allowance: Standard Information for A-Day)

Transport and General Workers Union (Legal Department)

Sue Ward

July 2005

Why pensions are so important

People are living longer...

If you were a man aged 65 in 1950, on average you could expect to live another 12 years. Today when you reach that age, you can expect an average of 19 years' additional life. It is estimated that a man reaching 65 in 2030 (who is aged 40 today) will have another 21 years to live on average. Women's life expectancy is higher than men's (although the gap is closing slowly), so a woman aged 65 today already on average has another 22 years to live. (The source of these figures is the report *Pensions: Challenges and Choices*, published by the government-sponsored Pensions Commission in 2004, which has a wealth of interesting statistics about the state of pensions in the UK today.)

Most of us would consider the opportunity of a longer life in retirement to be very good news – at least, so long as we knew we would have enough money to live on and enjoy ourselves. But the longer we live, the more money we are going to need for this.

Some other points worth bearing in mind are:

- These figures are *averages*. So while there are people who live a shorter time than this, there are also others who live a great deal longer. Of women reaching 65 this year, half can expect to live to 88, and a quarter to 94.
- Although government estimates of life expectancy are the best available at any one time, they are just that, estimates. Over the last 20 years, history has shown each set of updated official projections to be *under*-estimates. So we could be looking at considerably longer average life expectancy even than the figures above.

- Because of women's longer life expectancy, they tend to outlive their husbands or partners. In 2001, more than two-thirds of men over 65 were married, and only 17 per cent were widowers. Among women over 65, only 40 per cent were married, and 47 per cent widowed. While these figures will change as the gap between men's and women's life expectancies lessens, still there will be a very large group living as widows, perhaps for many years. There will also be rising numbers of people over 65 who have divorced and not remarried, or who have never married but had partners for differing periods of time.

So, uncomfortable as it is to do, people (especially women) need to think about their position in retirement in terms of not only what they will live on as a couple, but also what they will inherit, or have in their own right, if they once again become single. There are all too many poor pensioners, and elderly widows are the poorest of the poor.

Getting by or enjoying retirement?

Serious poverty among pensioners has been reduced in recent years, largely because of the Government's emphasis on providing means-tested benefits such as Pension Credit (see pages 79–80). It is still there, however, and so is the inequality between those at the top of the income scale and the rest. Figures from the Pensioners' Incomes series show that, in 2003–2004, 69 per cent of pensioner households depended on State benefits for at least 50 per cent of their income.

Only around 20 per cent of the pensioner population can really be considered affluent, and this figure is not likely to increase – indeed, it will probably decrease, unless three things happen, in some combination:

- State pensions go up in line with earnings (currently, because they are linked only to prices and not earnings, they are going down over time relative to the incomes of those in work);

- people work longer; and
- more money goes into non-State pensions and saving for retirement.

Currently, government policy appears to be based on the idea of increasing the levels of Pension Credit in line with earnings, but not State pensions. However, despite the Government's efforts at repackaging and re-presenting the Pension Credit, it is still a means-tested benefit, and many people hate the idea of claiming such benefits. One recent survey found that over a third of lower-income people not claiming Pension Credit said that nothing would induce them to apply for it (although this figure did go down when various incentives were offered).

There are a number of proposals for reform of State pensions, but as things stand, the State benefits you build up as of right, from your National Insurance contributions and credits (explained on pages 46–49), are low and expected to fall still further compared with the income of those in work. Relying on these National Insurance benefits will not give enough to live on, so you would need to apply for Pension Credit and other means-tested benefits. If you want to go above that level and have a comfortable retirement, you will need resources other than the State pension.

The keys to successful retirement provision are:

- not assuming you *have* to stop work at State Pension age;
- increasing the proportion of your current income that you put aside; and
- making sure that the money set aside is working as efficiently as possible for you.

Clearly, bad luck or changing economic conditions can knock a hole in the best-laid plans. However, the more you have planned ahead, and the more carefully you review your plans at regular intervals to keep up to date as other things change, the better the chances of success.

Women and pensions

Women have particular problems with building up enough pension for a comfortable retirement, so it is even more important for a woman to think about her position early, and review it regularly:

- In general, women earn less than men, tend to have gaps in their working lives and therefore a shorter National Insurance record, and tend to live longer, often alone. So women need to take every opportunity to ensure an adequate income in retirement. You can contribute to a personal or stakeholder pension even if you have no earnings (or someone else can do so for you). This is well worth considering if you have a gap in employment, perhaps while you are bringing up a family.
- Many married women expect to rely at least partially on their husbands' pensions. They often also assume that, if anything should happen to their husbands, there will be a widow's pension for them. Sadly, many marriages do not last into retirement and the pension position on divorce can be complicated. State widows' pensions have also been reduced, so there will be less to rely on from that source.
- If you are living with someone to whom you are not married, you may regard yourself as being in just the same position but the law does not. Some employers' pension schemes will give the equivalent of a widow's pension to a 'dependant', but many do not. The State is especially rigorous in demanding a marriage certificate before it will pay out.
- Over the last decade, there has been pressure to treat men and women equally in pension terms. The process has brought

advantages for women, but also disadvantages. Younger women (those born after 6 March 1955) will see the age at which they can draw their State Pension rise to 65. Most employers' pension schemes already have equal retirement ages, and often this is 65 for both sexes.

The position of women is therefore covered throughout this book, with special issues highlighted as appropriate.

The aim of this book

This book is intended to give you the information you need at the point at which you become concerned about your pension. It is aimed at people of any age, but especially anyone over 40 or so, whether in a job, self-employed, or not in paid work.

Chapter 1, after this Introduction, is called 'Planning ahead', and highlights points where there may be decisions to make, or information to obtain in order to be well-prepared. It includes a checklist of points to think about/check out about your own position, and cross-refers to other parts of the book where they are explained in more detail. All through the book, there are sections and sentences marked

✳ Action Points

which link back to that list in Chapter 1, explain what the issue is, and suggest what you might do.

Chapter 2 covers the various types of State pension and also briefly describes the means-tested Pension Credit. Chapter 3 then looks at all the various types of non-State pension as a group, with the different categories and types explained. Chapters 4 and 5 then give more detail about the two main types – occupational pensions (set up and run by or on behalf of the employer) and personal/stakeholder pensions (where the employer may or may not take a hand in arranging them, but the individual has a contract with the provider, which is usually an insurance company).

We have tried to explain a complicated system in simple terms, but there is bound to be some jargon, and many issues are too detailed to be dealt with in depth. So there is a glossary (from the Plain English Campaign) and a list of addresses for further information at the back. The text also contains reference to other leaflets that are available.

Further information

The Department for Work and Pensions (DWP) has a series of leaflets and detailed booklets about different aspects of its benefits. The part of the DWP that deals with pensions and pensioners is called The Pension Service. It has a single telephone number on 0845 606 0265; if you ring this number you will be connected to the pension centre covering your area, and the staff there can answer queries and tell you about local services. Alternatively, you can find a postal and email address for your local centre at www.thepensionservice.gov.uk/contact (see page 261 for more details).

The Financial Services Authority (FSA), the government body which regulates financial services, has produced a number of useful publications to help people plan their financial future. Those who have not yet started a pension should look at the *FSA Guide to Saving for Retirement: Starting to Save*, while those who already have one should check the *FSA Guide to Saving for Retirement: Reviewing your Plans*. There is also a fact-pack especially for women, called *Piling on the Pounds: Getting your Finances into Healthy Shape*.

For more information, the FSA also publishes a number of other booklets, a series of factsheets and a CD-ROM on financial planning. All these publications are available free from the FSA Consumer Helpline on 0845 606 1234 or on its website at www.fsa.gov.uk/consumer

As you work through the FSA booklets, you will find a number of exercises designed to help you establish what your pension 'target' should be and how much you need to pay as contributions to achieve this target.

The FSA website also has a series of comparative tables for the different products on the market, showing the charges and other basic information. As well as showing some basic savings products, these cover personal and stakeholder pensions. They are available at www.fsa.gov.uk/tables

Payment rates, and statements about the law, are based on the situation as at 6 April 2005. There may have been later changes, so make sure you have up-to-date information before taking further action. The next edition of this book should be published in September 2006.

PLANNING AHEAD

We have put this chapter near the beginning of this book so that you do not miss it, but the detailed information about the points covered here is mostly included in later chapters, and we have cross-referred to the various sections as necessary. So you may want to read through this chapter to pick out the issues that are relevant to you, then go to the later chapters to look at them in more detail, and finally come back to this chapter to complete some of the checklists and follow up on the actions proposed.

However, the first two sections ('How much do you need in retirement?' and 'What will you have coming in?') will help put everything else in perspective and help you see how much of a priority it is that you deal with your pension situation.

HOW MUCH DO YOU NEED IN RETIREMENT?

Only someone very close to retirement can work out the answer to this question in money terms. Younger people simply cannot know what is going to happen to the rate of inflation between now and their retirement. You can, however, make some very broad estimates in 'real' terms (in other words, in terms of today's money), and then compare what you are setting aside with those figures. Because they are only broad estimates, and because your circumstances and expectations will change, it's helpful to review all the figures regularly – perhaps every 5 years when you are young, going up to every 3 years or so when you are 20 years off the date you expect to retire, and annually when it is 10 years ahead or less. You'll also find it useful to do a review when your circumstances change, perhaps because you are changing jobs, getting married or divorced, or taking on a new mortgage.

✳ Action Points

So put down a figure first for your current annual income:

£_____

and then another one for how much of that you spend each year:

£_____

You might prefer to take monthly figures, rather than annual ones, here and all the way through this exercise. However, if you do so, remember to take account of income or spending which comes in lumps at particular times of the year, rather than being spread evenly across the year. An example on the income side might be bonus or commission payments, and on the spending side your payments for your summer holiday.

If you are regularly spending more than your income, and have debts that are growing rather than reducing, it would be sensible to deal with that issue *first*, before you start thinking about your pension. If you can get your debts under control, so that you are no longer spending out on interest payments and overdraft fees, you can then use the same money to put aside for your retirement.

Next, work out roughly what proportion of your spending goes on:

Mortgage or rent, and other housing costs	
Work-related expenses	
Cost of bringing up children	
All other living expenses	

Having done that calculation, you will be in a better position to see, very roughly, how your spending might change when you retire while still maintaining a standard of living you feel comfortable with. Now think about:

- How will your costs change when you stop work? For example, you won't need to buy a season ticket, but if you have a company car, will you need to replace it?
- If you have a mortgage, when will it be paid off? Do you have other insurance policies where your payments are due to end at a specified date, and when will that be?
- What stage will your children (or grandchildren) be at by then? Will they still be an expense for you?
- What leisure activities do you enjoy and how might they change? If bungee-jumping and whitewater rafting are your thing, the chances are that you won't still be doing them in your 70s: if it's concerts, museums and walking, you may well be.

So you should now be in a position to give a rough estimate of the percentage of your current income you'll need to have a comfortable retirement, and to put a money figure on that:

£_____

WHAT WILL YOU HAVE COMING IN?

We can now look at the other side of the picture, and see what you might have coming in. For each of the various sorts of pension you may have, you will either receive automatically, or can ask for, an estimate of the benefits in terms of today's money.

✱ Action Points

So collect together the statements for:

- your State Pension (obtained by filling in form BR19, as explained on pages 61–63);
- any occupational pension – that is, one from your employer (in most cases these are sent out automatically once a year; ask your pensions administrator if you have not received one in the last 12 months); and
- any personal or stakeholder pension (again, you should have an annual statement).

You may have one (or more) Combined Pension Forecast statements which show State pensions and non-State pensions on the same piece of paper. If you have more than one, remember that although your State Pension will be shown on each, you only receive it once.

The statements may not be on the same basis or use the same assumptions about the future, so they need to be used with caution. They will, however, give you an idea about what you can expect.

Put down figures for what each of these shows:

Increasingly, people also think of their non-pension savings as being available to finance their retirement. So put down also:

- a total (as at today) for other savings or investments you see as being there for the long term – not just those for a rainy day or for treats. These could be in any sort of investment vehicle, because for this purpose it's not the form they take, but your intentions for them, that matter; and

- a figure for part of the value of your home, if you own it and seriously intend (and would be able to) realise that value when you retire. But think carefully about this. If you are living in a large house in or near London, in an attractive part of the country, liberating some of its value may not be too difficult. But if you are living in a small terraced house in an area with a depressed housing market, you may not be so lucky. If you *are* planning to sell your current home, think about where you are going to live afterwards. It's better to err on the side of caution rather than rely on something that may not happen.

For more information, if you have been thinking along the lines of 'my home is my pension', then read the Age Concern publication *Using Your Home as Capital* (see page 269) and the FSA Factsheet *Raising Money from Your Home* (the FSA contact details are on page 262).

Put down all these capital figures:

You then need to think about what these capital figures might produce as income. One rule of thumb is that you can draw £1 of income for around every £20 or £25 of capital, without diminishing the capital. If you don't mind spending the capital, you could be a little less cautious (but remember those life expectancy figures on page 9). So decide on a reasonable formula and put down a rough annual income figure from your capital (or a monthly figure, if you have been working on monthly figures throughout).

£_____

Now you are in a position to add together your estimated pension income and non-pension income, and see how they compare with what you need to live on.

HOW DOES IT LOOK?

Tick one of these statements:

- I'm well on course for a comfortable retirement;
- I'll just about get by at retirement; or
- I'm heading into poverty.

If it is either of the latter two, you'll probably want to think hard about how you can change the situation. There may be opportunities you have missed which will cost you nothing, or only a little, to take advantage of, and some of these are highlighted in the rest of this book. It's more likely, however, that improving your *future* position is going to mean deferring some *current* spending, and putting more away for your retirement.

Couples

For a single person, this exercise is relatively straightforward. For a couple, it's more complex. You might like to take it through twice, once together and once separately. When doing it separately, each partner needs to take account of:

- pensions/savings held in his or her own right;
- those they would inherit from the other (for example, a widow's/widower's/civil partner's pension for a married couple); and
- life insurance policies, provided they would still pay out in retirement. If the life insurance is part of an occupational pension scheme, then what is provided will change as soon as you retire, and will generally drop down to zero, or to a minimal 'funeral benefit' within five years (see page 155).

State benefits

These figures don't take account of what you may be able to claim as Pension Credit, Housing Benefit (HB) or Council Tax Benefit (CTB) (briefly explained on pages 79–82). In terms of today's money, if your total income is less than around £110 a week as a single person, or £170 a week for a couple, you'll probably be able to claim the guarantee element of the Pension Credit, and CTB and/or HB as well, depending on your housing costs. If your total income is less than £150 a week for a single person, or £220 a week for a couple, you may be entitled to the savings element of Pension Credit. There is also some extra entitlement for people who are disabled, or carers. By the time you come to retire, the figures may be considerably higher in real terms, because at present Pension Credit rates are going up in line with earnings. (General living standards will also have gone up, however, so the rates may *feel* no more generous than they are now.)

However, the means-tested benefits have not been included because:

- although Pension Credit and the other benefits are certainly bringing some welcome help to the poorer pensioners, they are still low compared with earnings (median earnings for full-time workers were estimated at £441 a week – nearly £23,000 a year – in April 2005), and below what many people would aspire to for a comfortable retirement;
- although the Government regards this as an old-fashioned attitude, many people continue to take the view that they don't want to rely on 'handouts' from the State. Do remember, however, that Pension Credit is paid for out of the taxes to which we all contribute, and is just as much a legal right for those who qualify, as the National Insurance-based State pensions; and
- rules may change and, especially if you are some way off retirement, it is difficult to know what the benefit situation will be when you do get there.

This book only provides details of ways of saving for retirement through the different *pension* arrangements. There are, however, other ways of making provision, such as:

- building up other forms of savings and investment;
- living on the income from rents from buy-to-let housing;
- building up a business which you sell at the time you retire, and then investing the proceeds; or
- selling your home, and investing the proceeds.

All of these have different implications for tax, security and regulation, and all need expert advice. None of them is covered in detail in this book. If you are thinking along these lines you may wish to look at the Age Concern publication *Your Taxes and Savings* (see page 269).

✳ CHECKLIST OF ACTION POINTS

This is a summary of all the Action Points that are included in different places throughout the various chapters. Look in the main text for further details.

When	Action to take
When first reviewing your pension	Work out roughly what proportion of your current income you would need for a comfortable retirement (see pages 18–22).
	If it is clear that your income is already less than your outgoings, postpone sorting out your pension until you have found a way of bringing it back into balance; you can then use the money you save on interest charges and overdraft fees to set aside for the future.
	Establish which type of pensions you have (State, occupational DB, occupational DC, personal, stakeholder).
	Bring together your various pension statements (State, occupational, personal); if any are out of date, ask for up-to-date copies (see pages 61–63), and add up the estimates they give (but make sure that you don't count the State Pension more than once).
	Look for pension calculators on your scheme's or provider's website, and at the FSA's website.
	Work out roughly what income you might expect from savings and investments which you see as long term, including any capital that you plan to draw down (see pages 245–246).
	Bring together all the figures and decide if you are on course for a comfortable retirement, will just about manage, or would be struggling (see pages 22–23).

When	Action to take
	Consider whether you would be entitled to claim Pension Credit and other means-tested benefits from the State or local authority (see pages 79–82).
	Go through your pension scheme's booklets, websites and policy documents to ensure you understand the benefits, for yourself and for your dependants.
	If contracted out of S2P via a COMP or personal/stakeholder pension: consider whether this is appropriate, and if necessary write to the provider to say you wish to contract back in (see pages 107–114).
	Think about the age at which you plan to retire, and whether you might want to work on (perhaps part-time) for a period beyond State Pension age (see pages 89–90).
	If you have been thinking 'my home is my pension': consider whether this is realistic, and read the Age Concern book *Using Your Home as Capital* and the FSA factsheet *Raising Money from Your Home* (see page 21).
	Fill in the nomination 'expression of wish' form about any lump-sum death benefit provided, and if relevant also for dependant's pension (see pages 154–155).
Before April 2006	Consider whether there is any chance that you might be affected by the new Lifetime Allowance; if so, consult an accountant or financial adviser about what sort of protection to opt for (see pages 123–127).
	Consider whether you have a right to a 'protected pension age' (see page 135); if so, make sure you understand the implications and have the necessary documents.
If you decide you need to do more about your pension	Check if there are any gaps in your National Insurance contribution record which you could fill by paying voluntary contributions and so improve your State Pension or if there are credits you could claim (see pages 46–48).

When	Action to take
	Check whether your employer has an occupational scheme or a stakeholder or group personal pension (GPP) arrangement that you could join but have not. If so, join unless you have a particular reason not to. If you have a choice of contribution rates, think about choosing the one that brings in the most money from your employer.
	Decide whether you can afford to put more contributions into a pension, and if so, what sort of pension (Added Years, AVCs, FSAVCs, personal or stakeholder pension).
	For Added Years or AVCs: get a quotation from your pension scheme administrator and check the conditions and costs; sign up for a reasonable amount (but don't overstretch yourself).
	For a personal or stakeholder pension: decide on whether to make a series of single payments, or sign up for regular payments; what investment pattern will suit you; and how you want to pay for the costs of advice (see pages 222–224).
	If consulting a financial adviser: look for two or three local ones, ask for a preliminary interview and then decide which one you want to work with.
	Consider whether a Self Invested Personal Pension (SIPP) might be of interest. Before taking the plunge, check set-up and ongoing costs, and think about how active a role you would want to take in the investment (see pages 214–215). Take independent financial advice, especially if you are attracted to the idea of putting residential property into your fund.
	If you run a small business: consider whether a SSAS might be useful to you (see pages 145–146). If it might be take specialist financial advice.

When	Action to take
If you are married or in a Civil Partnership	Check what provision there is in your pension scheme(s) for your spouse or civil partner.
If you are living with someone you are not married to	Check whether they will receive a survivor's pension from your pension scheme(s) if you should die; if not, decide what alternative provision you can make.
If you are a woman	*If born after 6 March 1950:* check on the DWP website to establish the age at which you will be able to draw the State Pension (see page 39).
	If paying the reduced-rate married women's contributions: consider whether it is worth changing to the full rate (see pages 51–53).
	Consider whether the pension scheme has discriminated against women in the past (for example, by excluding part-timers most of whom were women) and, if so, whether you are eligible to make an equal-treatment claim.
When reviewing your retirement plans	Get up-to-date estimates of your pensions, and carry out again the exercise of comparing the income you need in retirement with the income you are likely to get; decide if you need to set more aside, and decide the best way to do this.
	With an occupational (defined-contribution), personal/stakeholder, or AVC pension: review the investment options you have chosen, consider whether they are still suitable, and switch between funds if necessary.
	Think about whether your views have changed on the age at which you want to retire.
If the employer wants to change your pension arrangements	Check that your employer is complying with the consultation requirements, and make sure you put your point of view. Ask your union or the Pensions Advisory Service (TPAS) for help if you want to oppose the change.

When	Action to take
	If your consent is required before the change is valid: put it in writing whether you consent or not, and keep a copy for future reference.
If your occupational scheme is going to be wound up	Work with your colleagues to get your union or TPAS to help you through the legal technicalities.
If you have concerns about your pension	*For a complaint about an occupational scheme:* speak to TPAS first to check out the legal position; then go through the disputes procedure, if necessary with help from TPAS, and on to the Pensions Ombudsman if still not satisfied.
	If your concern is more general: get hold of the relevant scheme documents and study them. Consider asking the scheme administrator or one of the trustees to come to a meeting at your workplace.
	If you are worried that there might be irregularities: talk to Public Concern at Work before going to the Pensions Regulator.
	For a personal pension scheme: speak to TPAS first, then raise it with the Pensions Ombudsman, the FSA, or the Compliance Officer at the providers, depending on the nature of the complaint.
If you change your job	Check whether your new employer has an occupational scheme or a stakeholder or GPP arrangement that you could join. If so, join unless you have a particular reason not to. If you have a choice of contribution rates, think about choosing the one that brings in the highest contribution from your employer.
	Consider what to do about any previous pension – refund of contributions (if eligible), deferred pension, or transfer. Check any deadlines for transfers on favourable terms.
	If you are offered a reduced transfer value from the old scheme: establish the reasons for this, and consider whether it is better to take it now or leave it in the scheme in the hope that the position improves.

When	Action to take
	If you are being transferred between employers, and the change is covered by the TUPE regulations (see pages 178–179): check what new pension arrangements are being made, and decide whether to join the new scheme or GPP/stakeholder arrangement.
	If your new employer is not paying contributions to any pension arrangement: consider whether to take out a personal/stakeholder pension on an individual basis or to arrange for direct deductions from your salary into the employer's 'designated' stakeholder pension. Alternatively, for a personal or stakeholder pension, decide on whether to make a series of single payments or sign up for regular payments; what investment pattern will suit you and how you want to pay for the costs of advice. Then consult a financial adviser (see pages 222–226).
If you have a break in employment	*If it is because you have become a carer*: consider whether you need to apply for Home Responsibilities Protection (see pages 49–51), and, if so, claim each year.
	If you are in an occupational scheme: check if it is possible to make up arrears for a gap in employment (for example, for periods of unpaid maternity leave).
	Check whether there are penalties on stopping and restarting a personal pension, and whether there are ways of avoiding these.
	Decide whether you can afford to continue to make payments when you are not earning (or if someone else such as your spouse or partner can do so).
If you are working part-time or have low wages	*If your earnings are below the Lower Earnings Limit*: consider whether you can increase your hours enough to bring you above the limit, so that you start building up entitlement to the State Pension and to social security benefits (see pages 54–55).

When	Action to take
	If you have had a 'Deficiency Notice' from HM Revenue & Customs: consider whether you can afford to make up the gap in your NI contributions, and whether or not it is worthwhile (see pages 74–75).
	If you have not joined an employer's pension scheme or GPP because you feel you cannot afford it: work out what the cost would really be, after taking account of savings on tax and National Insurance, and see if there is a way to make the money available.
	If part-timers are not allowed to join the employer's pension scheme: check (with your union or an advice agency) whether the employer is breaking the law, and challenge it if so.
If you are working abroad	Check with the DWP's International Pension Centre what the position is in the country you are going to (see page 63). If you will not be covered by National Insurance or the equivalent, ask for additional payment from your employer so you can make contributions to another pension.
	Check the position on getting tax relief for contributions into your employer's occupational pension scheme (*If working for a UK company abroad*) or a personal or stakeholder pension while you are away.
	Make the necessary arrangements before you leave.
If you are getting divorced	Check what will happen with your State Pension (see pages 70–71).
	Discuss with your solicitors how to deal with your other pension entitlements in the financial settlement – is pension sharing, earmarking, or offsetting against other assets the best method (see pages 158–160)?

When	Action to take
If you want to retire early (before State Pension age and/or the normal retirement age set by your scheme)	Decide whether you can afford to retire without receiving any help from the State; if not, decide also whether you can meet the conditions for Jobseeker's Allowance (see pages 86–88), or if over 60 whether you would qualify for the guarantee element of Pension Credit (see pages 79–80).
	If you have a protected pension age (see page 135): check if this will apply, and what effect if any it will have on the pension you can draw without tax penalty.
	If in an occupational scheme: establish what the conditions for taking early retirement are, and how much your pension would be reduced for early payment.
	If you have been paying AVCs: find out if you can start to draw them early, and how much they would be reduced for early payment.
	If you have a personal or stakeholder pension: establish what the conditions are for drawing it early, and decide whether you need to do this or can afford to wait.
If you need to take early retirement because of ill-health	Apply for Incapacity Benefit from the DWP (see pages 83–85).
	If in an occupational pension scheme: look in your scheme booklet for details of the ill-health benefit, and ask the scheme administrator how to apply; co-operate with their (reasonable) requests for information (see pages 185–186).
	If you have been paying AVCs: find out if you can start to draw them early, and how much they would be reduced for early payment.

When	Action to take
	If your request is unjustifiably rejected: go through the disputes procedure internally and then, if necessary, to the Pensions Ombudsman (see pages 199–200).
	If you have a personal or stakeholder pension: establish what the conditions are for drawing it early, and decide whether you need to do this or can afford to wait.
	If buying an annuity: check whether your state of health means you can buy an 'impaired life' annuity (see page 240).
If you plan to work beyond State Pension age	Consider whether to draw your State Pension or defer it, and, if you do want to defer, whether to take it as an increased benefit or a lump sum (see pages 75–79).
	Check how far your earnings will affect any means-tested entitlement and how much you are gaining by working.
	If in a public sector pension scheme: check if there are 'abatement' rules, how they will affect you, and how you can avoid their impact (see pages 187–188).
As you approach State Pension age (whether retiring or not)	Consider whether to draw your State Pension or defer it, and, if you do want to defer, whether to take it as an increased benefit or a lump sum (see pages 75–79).
	If you want to draw the State Pension, fill in and return the claim form three months before you reach State Pension age; remember that each person in a couple needs to make a separate claim (see pages 72–73).
When you retire	Check with The Pension Service, or a local advice agency, whether you would be eligible for Pension Credit, Housing Benefit and Council Tax Benefit, and claim if you are eligible (see pages 79–82).

When	Action to take
	If in an occupational DB scheme: decide how much of the pension you want to take as a lump sum. Consider how far this will reduce your income, how good a bargain it is, and what you plan to do with the lump sum (see pages 140–142).
	If in an occupational DC scheme or a personal pension: decide whether you want an annuity or an unsecured pension (see pages 226–239).
	If you decide on an annuity: consider what sort of annuity you want. Check if advice or help is available via your workplace or, if not, whether you should seek advice. Also consider the possibility of a short-term annuity (see page 128) as a form of unsecured income.
	If you decide on an unsecured pension: take specialist financial advice, and check what level of investment return you would need to make up for the loss of annuity income (see page 245–246).
	If retiring abroad: establish the position with drawing your State Pension in the country to which you are going, and make the necessary arrangements (allow ample time). Check also the position with having any occupational or personal pension paid abroad, and the costs of currency conversion.
Every few years in retirement, and certainly at age 75	*If taking an unsecured pension*: consider whether your decision is still correct, and review the investments and the income you are receiving (see pages 245–246).
	Check with The Pension Service, or a local advice agency, whether you are now eligible for Pension Credit, Housing Benefit and Council Tax Benefit, and claim if you are now eligible (see pages 79–82).

STATE PENSIONS

Nearly everyone pays National Insurance contributions towards their State Pension at some point in their lives, and most people can expect to receive something from the State when they retire. This chapter looks at all aspects of State pensions, including how the different parts of the State Pension work. It also explains about pensions in different circumstances, such as if you are divorced or widowed; drawing your pension; and increasing your pension by paying voluntary contributions or deferring drawing it. It also covers State benefits in retirement, including a brief summary of Pension Credit.

HOW STATE PENSIONS WORK

The State Pension comes in a number of parts. There is a flat-rate Basic Pension, and an earnings-related Additional Pension on top, previously called the State Earnings-Related Pension Scheme (SERPS), but now the State Second Pension (S2P). The way it was calculated has also changed but SERPS benefits already built up are safeguarded.

There is also a small Graduated Pension, for anyone who paid graduated National Insurance contributions between April 1961 and April 1975, and a 'non-contributory' pension for people aged 80 or more. All these are taxable.

Running alongside this is Pension Credit, a State benefit which is payable to those who have only modest income or savings. It is estimated that around half the pensioner population are currently eligible to claim. This book briefly summarises the way that Pension Credit works, but for fuller information see the Age Concern annual publication *Your Rights* (see page 269).

STATE PENSION AGE

People often talk about State retirement age, but in fact there is no such thing. You are not required to retire when you start drawing State Pension, and on the other hand you can be retired to all intents and purposes, but still have no entitlement to a State Pension because you are not old enough.

The *minimum* age at which a man can draw the State Pension is currently 65 for a man, 60 for a woman. Until April 2005, the age at which you *had* to start drawing it, if you were not to lose out, was 70 for a man, 65 for a woman. After April 2005, you can defer drawing your State Pension for as long as you want, and receive either a bigger pension or a lump sum in return (see pages 75–78 for details). Alternatively, you can work and draw the State Pension at the same time, although you will be taxed on both your earnings and the pension.

Women and State Pension age

Currently, women can start drawing the State Basic Pension at 60, while men have to wait until 65. However, women's State Pension age is going up to 65. The change is being phased in between April 2010 and March 2020. Women born before April 1950 will be unaffected, as they will already have reached 60 before the changeover period starts. Younger women will be able to claim their State Pension at 60 plus an extra month for every month (or part of a month) by which their birth date falls after 5 April 1950. A woman with a birth date of 6 April 1951, for example, will have to wait until she is 61 and one month old, becoming entitled on 6 May 2012. Any woman born after 6 March 1955 will not be able to draw the State Pension until she is 65.

✱ Action Points

To find the earliest date on which you will be able to draw a State Pension, look at the DWP website at www.thepensionservice.gov.uk/resourcecentre/home/ statepension/calc.asp
If you send for a State Pension forecast (see pages 61–63) this will also tell you what your State Pension date is.

CIVIL PARTNERSHIPS AND STATE BENEFITS

In 2004 Parliament passed the *Civil Partnerships Act*, which created a new type of legal relationship for same-sex partners. Civil Partnership registration ceremonies will be able to take place from December 2005 onwards, and, for social security purposes, those who have gone through them will be treated in the same way as an opposite-sex married couple.

When Civil Partnerships are introduced, State Pension provisions that currently apply to both husbands and wives will also apply to registered civil partners. However, where provisions apply only to women, such as the married woman's pension, rules will only be extended to civil partners when State Pension age starts to be equalised for men and women in 2010 (when they will also apply to married men). Same-sex couples who are living together but have not registered as civil partners will not be able to claim these benefits. This is in line with the law on opposite-sex couples living together without being married.

The law is different for means-tested benefits such as Pension Credit. For opposite-sex couples, and same-sex couples also once Civil Partnership comes into law, what matters is whether the couple are 'living together', not whether they have a legal marriage/Civil Partnership. So same-sex couples who have been living together for some time, and each claiming benefits in their own right, may find that the social security office challenges their position after December 2005. If they are required to claim as a couple, their benefits will be reduced from the previous level.

Gender Recognition Act 2004

Under this Act, people who have changed sex will be able to go through the process of having their acquired gender recognised by the Gender Recognition Panel. When they claim State benefits, the principle is that these will be paid according to their acquired gender, not their original one. So, for example, a man who has become a woman will also acquire the appropriate State Pension age.

While the process of gender recognition is going on, an existing spouse can apply for annulment of their marriage. If they don't do this, the marriage remains in force, and spouse's benefits and bereavement benefits continue as before.

For more information, see the website at www.grp.gov.uk

BASIC PENSION

The State Basic Pension is payable at the same rate to everyone who has reached State Pension age and meets the National Insurance contribution conditions. The full weekly rates from April 2005 to April 2006 are:

Single person	£82.05
Wife on husband's contributions	£49.15
Married couple on husband's contributions	£131.20
Married couple if both paid full contributions	£164.10

A reduced amount is payable if you do not have a full National Insurance contribution record, as explained on pages 44–46.

The Government announces each autumn how much the rates will increase the following April. The level of increase depends on the rise in the Retail Prices Index (RPI) for the year up to the previous September, but the Government has promised that it will be at least 2.5 per cent even if the increase in the RPI is less.

State Pensions for married women

If you are a married woman and you have paid full NI contributions for all of your working life, you should be entitled to a full State Basic Pension when you reach State Pension age. If you have paid full contributions for only part of your working life, you may be entitled to a reduced pension. Any years when you were paying the married woman's reduced-rate contributions (see pages 51–53) do not count towards a pension in your own right.

If you have not paid enough contributions to qualify for a pension in your own right, you will have to rely on your husband's contribution record. You can draw the married woman's pension, currently £49.15 a week, when your husband is 65, provided he does not decide to defer drawing his pension. However, if he does not have a complete contribution record, you too may get less than the full amount.

If the pension based on your own contributions is less than £49.15, it will be made up to a maximum of this amount when your husband draws his pension. If your own pension is more than this, you cannot get any extra pension based on your husband's contributions.

This is because of a general rule within the social security system called the 'overlapping benefits' rule. This rule says that if you have a potential entitlement to two benefits at the same time, you receive only the higher of the two, and not both.

Increases for dependants

Dependent wives

If you are under 60 when your husband draws his pension (at 65 or over), he may be able to claim an increase of £49.15 a week for you. However, he may not be able to receive this increase if you receive another State benefit of £49.15 or more or have earnings of over £56.20 a week, after certain expenses connected with work have been deducted. An occupational or personal pension counts as earnings for this purpose. If you are separated from your husband, he can still claim the increase for you but the earnings limit is £49.15 a week.

The State Pension a woman receives, whether based on her own or her husband's contributions, counts as her income for tax purposes.

If a husband receives a dependant's increase for his wife, paid with his pension, this will be taxed as part of his income.

Dependent husbands

If your wife is receiving a State Pension, she may be able to get an increase for you if she was receiving an addition for you with Incapacity Benefit immediately before she started drawing her pension. But she will not receive any increase if you have earnings of over £56.20 a week or receive a State Pension or certain other benefits of £49.15 or more.

The dependency rules will be equalised, and the conditions made the same as for dependent wives, at the same time as women's State Pension age is increased, from 2010 onwards.

Who qualifies for the Basic Pension?

First, you must have reached State Pension age. You then need to claim your pension. About four months before your State Pension age, you should be sent a retirement pack.

Second, The Pension Service looks back at the records of your National Insurance contributions over the whole of your working life. Before 1975, contributions were made by putting a stamp on a card each week. Since 1975, for employees they have been made through a percentage deduction from pay, collected via the tax system. Self-employed people pay a flat-rate contribution to the National Insurance Contributions Office (NICO) with an extra earnings-related element payable with their tax bill.

To get any State Basic Pension at all, you must, at some point in your working life, have paid *either* 50 weekly NI stamps in the pre-1975 system *or* enough earnings-related NI contributions in any year since

1975 to make it a 'qualifying year'. This is known as the 'first contribution condition'. For the 'second contribution condition', NI credits also count – see below for details.

To get a full Basic Pension you must have paid or been credited with NI contributions for most of your 'working life', as explained in the next section.

Normally you need to have satisfied the contribution conditions in your own right, but married women, divorcees and widowed people may be able to claim a pension on their spouse's or former spouse's contribution records. Pensions for divorced people are explained on pages 70–71 and for widowed people on pages 65–70.

Your working life

Your 'working life' is the period on which your NI contribution record is based. It normally starts in the tax year during which you reach 16. It ends with the last full tax year before your State Pension age or the last full tax year before your death (this is important for the calculation of bereavement benefits). The normal working life is therefore currently 49 years for a man (16–65) and 44 years for a woman (16–60). This will change from 2010 onwards for women, and by March 2020 it will also be 49 years for a woman.

Qualifying years

A 'qualifying year' is a tax year in which you have paid (or been credited with) contributions on sufficient earnings to count towards your pension record. The rules about what constitutes a qualifying year have changed a number of times.

For years up to 1975, all your NI stamps and credits are added up and divided by 50, rounding up any that are left over. But you cannot have more qualifying years worked out in this way than the number of years in your working life up to April 1975.

Since 1975 contributions have been based on a percentage of earnings and collected through the tax system. Between 1975 and 1978 a qualifying year was one in which you paid or were credited with contributions on earnings of at least 50 times the weekly Lower Earnings Limit (LEL). This is usually around the level of the Basic Pension and is the minimum level of earnings that qualifies for contributory benefits. Since 1978, a qualifying year has been one in which you had earnings of at least 52 times the weekly LEL.

To receive a full Basic Pension, about nine out of every ten years in your working life need to be qualifying years, according to a scale laid down by the DWP.

Length of working life	Number of qualifying years needed for a full Basic Pension
41 years or more	Length of working life minus 5
31–40 years	Length of working life minus 4
21–30 years	Length of working life minus 3
11–20 years	Length of working life minus 2
1–10 years	Length of working life minus 1

If you have fewer qualifying years than this, you will be paid a reduced Basic Pension. The minimum pension actually payable is 25 per cent of the full rate. The table overleaf shows the percentage of the full pension for which you would qualify, assuming your working life is the full 44 years (women) or 49 years (men).

Number of qualifying years	Percentage of the full Basic Pension for which you qualify	
	Women	Men
9 or less	0	0
10	26	0
11	29	25
15	39	35
20	52	46
30	77	69
39	100	89
44 or more	100	100

Example

Christine was born on 10 August 1947 and was 16 in 1963. Her working life runs from 6 April 1963 to 5 April 2007, a total of 44 years. To receive a full Basic Pension, she needs 39 or more qualifying years. If she has worked and paid, or been credited with, contributions for only 20 years of her working life, she will receive just over half the Basic Pension.

National Insurance contributions and credits

There are several different types of NI contribution.

Class 1

Class 1 contributions are paid by employees and their employers. There are three important earnings levels. These are:

- the Lower Earnings Limit (LEL)
- the Earnings Threshold (ET)
- the Upper Earnings Limit (UEL)

The table below shows what these are, in weekly, monthly and annual terms, during 2005–2006:

	LEL	ET	UEL
Weekly	£82	£94	£630
Monthly	£356	£408	£2,730
Annual	£4,264	£4,895	£32,760

The way the system works is:

- If you earn less than the LEL, you do not pay any National Insurance contributions, but neither are you building up a National Insurance record to help you qualify for National Insurance benefits.
- If your earnings are between the LEL and the ET, you still do not pay any National Insurance, but your earnings above the LEL are counted for NI purposes as if you are paying. (Technically, you are considered as paying NI but at a rate of 0 per cent.)
- If you are earning above the ET, but less than the UEL, you pay a percentage of all your earnings above the ET in National Insurance, and all your earnings above the LEL are counted for NI purposes. The percentage you pay depends on whether you are 'contracted in' or 'contracted out' of S2P via an employer's pension scheme (explained on pages 107–114).
- If you are earning more than the UEL, for the main NI contribution you are treated as if you are only earning the same amount as the UEL (a maximum of £630 a week this tax year). You pay a 1 per cent contribution on your earnings above the UEL (this is a special additional contribution imposed by the Government in 2003 to pay for extra spending on the NHS).

The *employer's* NI contributions start at the ET (£94 a week in 2005–2006) and there is no ceiling on them. Again, the rate depends on whether the employee is contracted in or out of S2P, and in this case also by what method (explained on pages 107–114).

Reduced-rate contributions for married women are considered on pages 51–53.

Class 2

Class 2 contributions are flat-rate contributions paid by self-employed people (currently £2.10 a week in 2005–2006). They count towards the Basic Pension but not towards S2P. Self-employed married women who chose to pay reduced-rate contributions when they were available, and have never changed to the full rate, pay no Class 2 contributions.

Class 3

Class 3 contributions are flat-rate voluntary contributions. They are £7.35 a week in 2005–2006. (See pages 74–75 for information about when it may be wise to pay these.)

Class 4

Class 4 contributions are paid by self-employed people at a rate of 8 per cent on profits between lower and upper limits (£4,895 and £32,760 in 2005–2006 – there is also a 1 per cent contribution on profits above £32,760). These contributions do not entitle you to any extra benefit, however.

Credits

Men between the ages of 60 and 65 who do not have any earnings receive 'autocredits' (in other words, they are automatically treated as if they have paid NI contributions), unless they are self-employed or are abroad for more than half the year. (This will also apply to women once they have the same State Pension age as men.)

Credits can take the place of NI contributions in certain other circumstances also. The main ones are:

- if you are registered for Jobseeker's Allowance and seeking work (so it may be worth registering even if you do not qualify for any benefit);

- if you are unable to work because you are sick or disabled;
- if you are receiving Working Tax Credit (in some cases); or
- if you are receiving Carer's Allowance (previously called Invalid Care Allowance).

✳ Action Points

Check whether you are eligible for any of these credits, or if you qualify for Home Responsibilities Protection (explained below), before spending your own money on Class 3 contributions.

In some cases you may need to write to NICO to claim a credit. Check with the social security office at the time whether this applies to you.

Home Responsibilities Protection

Before 1978 a woman (or a man) who stayed at home to bring up children or look after a relative would have a gap in their NI contribution record which affected their State Pension. The system of Home Responsibilities Protection (HRP), introduced in 1978, reduces the number of qualifying years you need in order to qualify for a full Basic Pension. However, it covers complete tax years only, and does not include any years before 1978. A married woman or widow cannot get HRP for any tax year in which, if she was working, she would only be due to pay reduced-rate NI contributions (see pages 51–53).

You are entitled to HRP if you meet any of the following conditions, or a combination of them, for a whole tax year:

- You are the 'main payee' for Child Benefit for a child under 16. This applies equally to a woman or a man who stays at home to care for children. If it is the man who stays at home, he will need to apply to become the 'main payee', as this is normally the woman. If you have more than one child, each parent in a couple can be a main payee, so safeguarding both people's pension rights.

- You get Income Support and are not required to register for Jobseeker's Allowance because you are looking after someone.
- For at least 35 hours a week you look after someone who receives Attendance Allowance, the middle or higher rate of the care component of Disability Living Allowance, or Constant Attendance Allowance.
- You are a foster parent (for years from 2003–2004 onwards).

For years up to 5 April 1988 you needed to fulfil the third condition for the full tax year, but from 6 April 1988 you must have been caring for at least 48 weeks a year. (If you receive Carer's Allowance, you will normally be given automatic credits towards your pension instead.

Each year of 'home responsibility' is taken away from the number of qualifying years you need to get a full pension. Even with HRP, however, you must normally have at least 20 qualifying years to qualify for a full Basic Pension. If you have fewer than this, you may be able to get a pension at a reduced rate.

Example

Sheela started work at 16 and paid full-rate NI contributions for 29 years. She then gave up work to look after her mother. Sheela's Basic Pension is worked out as follows:

Working life	44 years
Number of qualifying years normally needed for full pension	39 years
Number of years HRP	15 years
Number of years needed for full pension after taking away HRP years	24 years

As Sheela has the full number of qualifying years, she gets the full Basic Pension.

✳ Action Points

HRP will be given automatically if you qualify under either of the first two conditions referred to above. However, you need to make a claim if you qualify under the third condition, or if you qualify under one condition for part of the tax year and under another for the rest of the year.

If you are a man who is at home looking after children, make sure you have arranged to be the 'main payee' of Child Benefit for at least one child. If you apply within the first three months of a tax year, this will take effect for the whole of that year. Otherwise, it will not be effective until the next year.

For years spent caring between 1978 (when the system started) and April 2002, you can claim at any time up to State Pension age. For years from April 2002, however, you must claim after the end of the relevant tax year, and within three years of the end of it.

The DWP computer cannot accept 'running claims', so you need to ensure that you claim for each year that counts. It could be wiser to make one claim each year after 6 April, rather than save up your claims and send them in every three years. Ask for claim form CF411 from the DWP after the end of any tax year when your earnings have not gone above the annual Lower Earnings Limit.

Married women's reduced-rate contributions

Until 1977, married women and widows who worked for an employer, and earned more than the Lower Earnings Limit, could choose to pay reduced-rate National Insurance contributions. Since 1977, it has not been possible to choose to start paying at this reduced rate. However, women who had already taken up the option before then can continue to do so, unless they have a break in their employment for two or more complete consecutive tax years. The rate is now 4.85 per cent of earnings between the Earnings Threshold and the Upper Earnings Limit.

> **Example**
>
> **Angela** has been paying reduced-rate NI contributions for many years, but she lost her job in May 2004. She will be able to continue to pay the reduced rate if she gets another job at any time before 6 April 2007. But if the gap is longer than that, she will have to pay at the full rate when she goes back to work.

A widow who remarries can continue to pay reduced-rate contributions after her marriage. You should send a certificate of election (CF383) with your marriage certificate to your social security office. This certificate also allows you to continue to pay reduced-rate contributions if you change jobs.

You cannot, however, continue with reduced-rate contributions if your marriage ends in divorce or annulment. You must then pay full-rate contributions from the date of either decree.

Class 3 voluntary NI contributions (see page 48) cannot be paid to cover the same period during which reduced-rate contributions have been paid. Nor can you get Home Responsibilities Protection (see pages 49–51) for any year when you have chosen to pay reduced-rate contributions.

Reduced-rate NI contributions give you no benefits in your own right. If it is to be worth changing to full-rate contributions, however, you need to be able to build up sufficient 'qualifying years' to give you a worthwhile pension. You will in any case be entitled to the married woman's pension (about 60 per cent of the full Basic Pension) once your husband draws his pension at or after the age of 65 (depending on his contribution record). So if you are five or more years younger than your husband, it is likely to be worthwhile only if you can build up your pension to more than 60 per cent of the full amount. If the age gap is smaller, or you are older than your husband, it may be worth ensuring that you have some State Pension of your own, even if it is not very much. If you are earning between the LEL and the ET (explained on pages 46–47) it will not in fact cost you anything at all, because NI contributions for this band of earnings are at a zero rate. But remember that you can never change back to the reduced rate.

The National Minimum Wage (NMW) is £5.05 an hour from October 2005, while the ET is £94 a week for 2005–2006. So if you are working fewer than 18.6 hours a week at the NMW, you will fall into this band.

The younger you are now, the more likely it is to be worth making the change. You are less likely to benefit if you are in your 50s, are younger than your husband, and have not paid NI contributions regularly in the past. It may be worthwhile to start paying at the full rate even if you will not qualify for State Basic Pension, since:

- Full-rate contributions will enable you to qualify for benefits such as Jobseeker's Allowance and Incapacity Benefit (although there is a time-lag of over two and a half years before you are entitled to these).
- You will be given NI credits for periods of sickness or unemployment.
- You will be able to get Home Responsibilities Protection if you fulfil the other conditions.
- You may be able to pay Class 3 voluntary contributions to cover gaps in your contribution record.
- You may qualify for some S2P even if you do not qualify for a Basic Pension, as the contribution conditions are different.

For more information, see HMRC leaflets CA13 *National Insurance Contributions for Married Women with Reduced Elections* and CA09 *National Insurance Contributions for Widows or Widowers.*

✳ Action Points

Send for a State Pension forecast (see page 61–63) to see what your pension entitlement would be.

If your date of birth is later than 6 April 1950, check what age you will be when you are allowed to draw the State Pension before you make the decision (see page 39).

Ask for advice from your local social security office or Citizens Advice Bureau if you are not sure whether to change to paying full-rate contributions.

Working part-time

Many women (and a few men) with home responsibilities take up part-time work, often badly paid, and without any pension entitlement from their employer. If you are earning below the LEL (£82 a week or £4,264 a year in 2005–2006) you pay nothing – nor are you building up qualifying years for your Basic Pension. As soon as you earn above that level, you are building up NI entitlement, but you do not now start paying contributions until you reach the Earnings Threshold (£94 a week or £4,895 a year in 2005–2006).

If you have more than one job, and each one gives you earnings below the LEL, you will not pay NI contributions on any of them, nor build up any pension entitlement however much your earnings are in total.

If you qualify for Home Responsibilities Protection (see pages 49–51), you will get this, provided that any earnings you have within the tax year are less than the annual LEL for that year. If you do not qualify for HRP, then HM Revenue & Customs should send you a statement, about 15–18 months later, telling you how many Class 3 (voluntary) contributions you need to make to turn the year into a qualifying year.

Part-time work and low pay also affect any entitlement you might have to SERPS/S2P: your lifetime average earnings could be lower than for someone who has worked full-time and then taken a career (or other) break.

As explained on page 58, S2P gives much more to those earning between the Lower Earnings Limit and the top of Band 1 (£4,264 and £12,100 in 2005–2006) than SERPS did, and someone earning only just above the LEL will be treated as if they are earning £12,100. This could make it worthwhile increasing your hours to bring you above the LEL.

✳ Action Points

Check what your earnings were, and whether they were below the LEL, in the last tax year. If they were, have you had a 'Deficiency Notice' from HM Revenue & Customs, about paying voluntary contributions? Before you make up your mind whether to do so or not, look at HMRC leaflet CA93 *Short Fall in your NICs: National Insurance Contributions: To Pay or Not to Pay?*

If your earnings are still below the LEL this year and you have children under six, or you are a carer, you will be getting a credit towards S2P. If not, think about changing your job or increasing your hours to bring you just above that level. Annual earnings of £4,200 (in 2005–2006) mean that you pay no NI contributions, but you build up no State Basic or Second Pension either. Annual earnings of £4,300 (in 2005–2006), however, still mean that you pay no NI contributions, but you are helping to build up State Basic Pension entitlement, and for S2P you are treated as if you are earning £12,100.

ADDITIONAL PENSION

As well as the State Basic Pension, there is also a State Additional Pension. From April 2002 onwards, rights to Additional Pension are being built up under the scheme as State Second Pension (S2P), but all Additional Pension rights built up before that date under the State Earnings-Related Pension Scheme (SERPS) remain in place.

Who qualifies?

In order to have any S2P (or SERPS before it) you must have paid Class 1 NI contributions for employees (explained on pages 46–47) or, for S2P only, be covered by the special provisions for carers or disabled people explained below. You do not build up entitlement during years when you are self-employed and paying Class 2 contributions. Widows and widowers may qualify for SERPS and S2P on their spouse's contributions. It is possible to have some pension from SERPS or S2P, even if you do not qualify for any Basic Pension.

How does S2P work?

Your S2P (and SERPS before it) depends on your 'band earnings' or 'reckonable earnings' during your working life. These are earnings between the Lower and Upper Earnings Limits for each tax year from 1978–1979 until the year before you reach State Pension age. The 2005–2006 weekly limits are £82 and £630. So if you earn £300 per week in 2005–2006, your band earnings will be £300 – £82 = £218.

S2P/SERPS is calculated by first revaluing your band earnings for past years in line with rises in national average earnings, according to an index produced by the DWP. Your band earnings for each year are then added together, and averaged.

The various rates change each year, and may be very different by the time you come to retire. In today's money, however:

- Any employees whose 'band earnings' are less than £12,100 a year but more than the Lower Earnings Limit (£4,264) will be treated under S2P as if their earnings are £12,100.

- Many carers will also be credited into the scheme as though they had earnings of £12,100 a year.

People who are looking after a child, up to the end of the tax yearbefore his or her sixth birthday, and anyone getting Carer's Allowance because they are looking after someone with disabilities, get automatic credits.

✳ Action Points

If you do not get Carer's Allowance but are looking after someone who receives Attendance Allowance, or if you receive Income Support, without having to sign on as a jobseeker because you are looking after someone with a disability, you will need to apply for credits.

For more information, see DWP leaflet PM9 *State Pensions for Carers and Parents: Your Guide.*

People with disabilities will also be credited for complete years when they were receiving Incapacity Benefit (IB) or Severe Disablement Allowance (SDA), *so long* as they worked and paid Class 1 NI contributions for at least one-tenth of their working life.

Calculating S2P

Calculating S2P is complex, and it links back to the way SERPS was calculated for years up to April 2002. Originally, there was only one band of earnings, between the Lower and Upper Earnings Limits (explained on page 47). Each year's earnings within that band were revalued in line with average earnings growth, and the total was then divided by 80, and multiplied by the number of years the person had been in SERPS since its start. If they had contributed to SERPS for the full 20 years, they received the maximum pension of $\frac{20}{80}$ (25 per cent) of their average revalued band earnings.

However, SERPS was cut back in 1986, with the changes beginning to come into effect in 1999–2000. The maximum SERPS Pension of 25 per cent began to be phased down by 0.5 per cent annually from the tax year 1999–2000, with the aim of reaching 20 per cent in 2009–2010. The way in which earnings were calculated also changed, so that revaluation applied to a smaller slice of earnings.

Under the State Second Pension, this phasing down has been carried on, but in addition the formula has been 'tilted' towards the lower paid. So there are now three bands of earnings rather than one. For anyone with a State Pension age of 6 April 2009 or later, the formula is:

- For earnings between the Lower Earnings Limit and the top of Band 1 (£12,100 a year in 2005–2006), whether this is the actual amount of your earnings or the notional amount for the purposes of this calculation, the pension is 40 per cent of the revalued earnings figure. Low-paid people will therefore receive considerably more than they would have received under SERPS.
- For earnings between £12,100 and £27,800 (Band 2), the pension is 10 per cent of the revalued earnings figure.
- For earnings over £27,800 up to the Upper Earnings Limit, the pension is 20 per cent of the revalued earnings figure, as it would have been under SERPS.

The reason for this peculiar formula is that when the Government made the changes in 2002, it wanted to give more to lower-paid people without the higher-paid either gaining or losing, and this arrangement achieves this.

For anyone retiring between 6 April 2000 and 5 April 2010, the 'phasing down' explained above makes the position much more complex, because the percentage is lower in each succeeding year. So for example for someone reaching State Pension age in 2008–2009, the structure is:

- Band 1 – 41% of earnings
- Band 2 – 10.25% of earnings
- Band 3 – 20.5% of earnings

After the new system has been running for about five years, there may be another reform to make the S2P largely flat-rate for people below a certain age: the cut-off point is likely to be 45. However, although this was proposed in the original Green Paper on pensions in 1998, little more has been heard about this plan and it is not clear whether the change will go ahead or not.

✳ Action Points

Social security leaflet NP46 *A Guide to State Pensions* gives detailed examples. Look at these if you are interested in seeing how the calculations are done. Alternatively – and more simply – you can find out your current and projected SERPS/S2P entitlement by filling in form BR19, as explained on pages 61–63.

Contracted in or out?

An employee who is building up a non-State pension (occupational, personal or stakeholder) may be either contracted-in or contracted-out of SERPS/S2P (this is explained on pages 107–114). The idea of contracting out is that your Additional Pension from SERPS/S2P is replaced, in whole or in part, by your non-State pension. However, in the early days of SERPS there was a guarantee that you could not lose out by being contracted-out, although this has now been almost completely eroded, and so many people who were contracted-out in the years up to 1997 will receive a limited amount of SERPS as well as their non-State pension, to make up any gap because the two were calculated in different ways.

In addition, when the Government altered SERPS to S2P, it was anxious to ensure that low-paid people were not disadvantaged by belonging to an occupational scheme which contracted out of S2P. So it has provided a top-up system. Anyone who has contracted out but is earning less than the top of Band 1 (£12,100 in 2005–2006) in a year will get their non-State pension topped up by a payment of S2P. The contracted-out salary-related pensions of people earning up to the top of Band 2 (£27,800 in 2005–2006) will also be topped up from the State. The relevant figures will be calculated and paid automatically by The Pension Service when the individual retires.

GRADUATED PENSION

As well as possibly having the Basic and Additional Pension, many people coming up to retirement find that they have a small amount of Graduated Pension. This comes from a scheme that lasted from April 1961 to April 1975. It was then frozen until 1978, but since then it has been inflation-proofed at the same rate as the Basic Pension.

The Graduated Pension is based on the number of 'units' paid between 1961 and 1975 and the value of a unit when the pension is claimed. Women get 9.93p per week for every £9 paid, men 9.93p per week for every £7.50 paid. Most people who receive Graduated Pension get less than £3 a week from it.

It is possible to qualify for a Graduated Pension even if you have not paid enough contributions to entitle you to the Basic Pension. However, there can be disadvantages in claiming it, as explained on page 76.

While the Graduated Pension scheme was running, there were 'contracting-out' arrangements for people who belonged to their employers' pension schemes. Contact the Pension Tracing Service (on 0845 600 2537 or at the address on page 262) if you have lost touch with your former employers and think they may have had a scheme.

OVER-80s PENSION

This is a non-contributory State Pension of £49.15 a week for people aged 80 or over who do not qualify for a Retirement Pension. For someone who already gets a Retirement Pension of less than this amount, an Over-80s Pension will be paid to bring their pension up to this level.

To qualify for this pension you have to be living in the UK on the day you become 80 or on the date of your claim if this is later, and to have been here for 10 years or more in any 20-year period since your 60th birthday. If you have lived in another European Union country (including Gibraltar), this may help you qualify.

For more information, see social security claim form (with notes) BR 2488.

Age-related additions

Once you reach 80 you receive 25p per week extra with your State Pension. If a husband and wife are both over 80, they each receive the extra amount.

PENSION FORECASTS

Anyone can get an estimate of what their State Pension will be, taking account of their contribution record so far, from the DWP. You can use the Internet (www.thepensionservice.gov.uk) to request and receive this online, or you can fill in the form (BR19) on-screen or by hand and post it. Alternatively, you can request a forecast by phone, on 0845 3000 168, or from the address on page 262.

The DWP warns that it needs to be sure of your identity when you make an application, so it may ask for official documents to support the information you give. It can take the Team up to eight weeks to send a forecast, after you send off the application form.

The forecast will tell you the amount to which you are already entitled, based on your contributions to date, and how much you will be entitled to at State Pension age, assuming you pay NI contributions until then. It explains what you might be able to do to get a better State Pension. For widowed or divorced people it tells you the amount of Basic, Additional and Graduated Pension you are entitled to, based on your former spouse's contributions.

The forecast also allows you to check what would happen to your State Pension in different situations, such as:

- working on after State Pension age (pages 89–90);
- retiring early (pages 82–89);
- going abroad (pages 63–64);
- paying at the full rate after paying reduced-rate contributions (pages 51–53);
- paying voluntary contributions to make up for those not paid in the past (pages 74–75); and
- getting married or divorced (pages 70–72).

It also shows what difference a change in your annual earnings would make, and whether there is anything you can do to improve your Basic State Pension.

Over the next few years, many employers and pension providers will begin providing brief information about your State Pension alongside details of the pensions they provide, in Combined Pension Forecasts. There are also plans for The Pension Service to provide State Pension statements automatically, but these will take some time to come fully into effect.

✳ Action Points

Get a copy of the State Pension Forecast form (BR19), fill it in and send it off. When you get an answer, if there is anything you don't understand or which appears to be incorrect, follow it up. (There are quite a number of mistakes in the National Insurance records, and it is much easier to sort them out while you are still at work than later.)

Make a note to carry on sending for forecasts every few years (more often as you get closer to retirement) and also to do so if there are major changes in your life – changing your job, stopping work, getting married or divorced.

PENSIONS ABROAD

Working abroad

If you work abroad but still officially live in this country, you usually have to pay NI contributions. If you work for a multinational company abroad, it will probably arrange to do this for you. If you are not 'domiciled' here, you will not need to pay UK contributions, but you may be required to contribute to your host country's social security benefit arrangements for benefits there. You can sometimes make voluntary (Class 3) contributions during periods of overseas service, but there are time limits for making them.

✳ Action Points

Before you go, check with the International Pension Centre (on 0191 218 7777) about the position in the country where you plan to work. There are special arrangements for 'migrant' workers within the European Union and a number of social security treaties with other governments. If for some reason you will not be covered, ask for additional payment from your employer so that you can make private arrangements.

Retiring abroad

If your pension is paid into a bank or other account, you do not need to tell your local office unless you are staying abroad for more than six months. You can, if you wish, arrange to receive your pension in the country where you are staying. In most countries, the payment is made monthly, direct into a bank in that country. This tends to be the most secure method, and would generally also mean a better exchange rate than with other methods. There are special payment arrangements for pensions in India, Pakistan and Bangladesh, and for New Zealand.

If you remain abroad, the annual pension increase will be paid only in a European Union country or in one of the countries with which the UK has special arrangements (Barbados, Bermuda, Bosnia-Herzegovina, Croatia, Gibraltar, Guernsey, Iceland, Israel, Jamaica, Jersey, Mauritius, Norway, Philippines, Sark, Slovenia, State Union of Serbia-Montenegro, and the former Yugoslav Republic of Macedonia, Switzerland, Turkey and the USA. In any other country, your State Pension will continue at the rate at which it was being paid when you left the UK. If you come back to the UK and re-establish residence, the pension will be increased to the full rate again.

✳ Action Points

Make sure you allow yourself ample time to establish the position, work out the implications for your finances, and make arrangements, especially if you are emigrating.

For more information, see social security leaflet GL29 *Going Abroad and Social Security Benefits* and HMRC leaflet NI38 *Social Security Abroad.*

PENSIONS FOR WIDOWS AND WIDOWERS

This section covers the benefits for widows and widowers (and bereaved civil partners once the new arrangements are in force – see pages 39–40) as they are today. However, anyone whose spouse died before 9 April 2001 will still be covered by the old benefit rules (which are covered briefly on page 69).

Bereavement Payment

You will receive a non-taxable single lump-sum Bereavement Payment of £2,000, provided that:

- your spouse/civil partner had the right National Insurance contributions in the past (most people will qualify under these conditions); and
- your spouse/civil partner was not receiving a State Pension when he or she died, or you are under State Pension age.

✳ Action Points

It is possible in some circumstances to make NI contributions after a death, to build up the deceased person's NI record so that the spouse/civil partner receives more. Check with the DWP to see if this applies.

Bereavement Allowance for those under State Pension age

If you are aged at least 45 when your spouse/civil partner dies but have not started to receive a State Pension, you should receive a Bereavement Allowance of up to £82.05 a week for 52 weeks. This is taxable. If your spouse/civil partner had not paid sufficient National Insurance contributions, you may not get the full amount. The contribution conditions are the same as for the State Pension (explained on pages 43–46). However, if your spouse/civil partner died as a result of an industrial accident or disease, there are no contribution conditions. Bereavement Allowance stops if you reach State Pension age or remarry while it is being paid.

If you are between 45 and 55 when your spouse/civil partner dies, you may receive a reduced 'age-related' rate, which is 7 per cent lower for each year by which you are younger than 55 (so that a 45-year-old receives only 30 per cent of the full rate). These rates are decided by the age at which you start to qualify and do not change as you get older. No Additional Pension inherited from your deceased spouse/civil partner (see below) is paid until you reach State Pension age.

People with dependent children

If you have dependent children when your spouse/civil partner dies, there is a Widowed Parent's Allowance whatever your age. This is £82.05, plus an addition for SERPS/S2P. There was previously also an allowance for each child but this was replaced for new claimants by the Child Tax Credit from April 2003.

A man who lost his wife before 9 April 2001, but who still meets the conditions, can also start claiming Widowed Parent's Allowance. However, it will not be backdated for more than three months from the date of your claim.

The Widowed Parent's Allowance is not affected by earnings. If you remarry you will lose the Widowed Parent's Allowance. It will also be suspended during any period when you live with someone else as husband and wife. It stops when the children are no longer dependent (which means at 16, or at 19 if still in full-time education).

However, a woman who was already drawing the (now abolished) Widowed Mother's Allowance on 9 April 2001 can move on to

Widow's Pension under the old rules (explained below), if she is over 45 when they stop being dependent.

Reaching State Pension age

Once a widow reaches 60, she can draw the State Basic Pension based on her deceased husband's contributions and/or her own. A widow's entitlement will be based on her husband's contribution record if this gives a better level of pension than her own. If she is 60 or over when her husband dies and not receiving a full Basic Pension, she may be able to use his contribution record to bring her Basic Pension up to the maximum for a single person. A widower can use his wife's contribution record in the same way. In general, this is only possible if both were over State Pension age when she died, but there are some exceptions to this, and men who are widowers when they reach State Pension age should seek advice. The discrimination against widowers will be ended when State Pension age starts to be equalised from 2010.

A widow will also receive half of her husband's Graduated Pension as well as any based on her own contributions.

A widow or a widower can also draw 'Inherited' SERPS and S2P, as explained below, if they have received one of the widow's or bereavement allowances at any time during their lives, and have not remarried since.

Inherited SERPS

As SERPS was originally designed, a widow inherited the whole of her husband's SERPS pension, so long as she was eligible for the basic Widow's Pension.

In 1986 the Government made a number of changes to SERPS. One of these was that if the husband's death occurred after 5 April 2000, the widow would inherit only half his SERPS pension. This also applies to widowers, where both are over State Pension age at the date of the wife's death. However, the DWP ignored this change in its leaflets about the subject, and in the letters officials sent to people, right up until April 1999. After much pressure from organisations concerned with pensions (including Age Concern), in 2000 the Government announced some protection for those close to or beyond State Pension age.

As a result of this:

- Men and women who reached State Pension age before 5 October 2002 are exempt from the changes. They can pass on all of their SERPS entitlement, as now.
- The new rules only apply in full to men and women who were 10 years or more away from State Pension age in October 2002.

For anyone within 10 years of their State Pension age in October 2002, the changes are being phased in. The table below shows how this works:

% SERPS passing to surviving spouse	Date when contributor reaches State Pension age (or would have done if they had not died earlier)
100%	3.10.2002 or earlier
90%	6.10.2002 – 5.10.2004
80%	6.10.2004 – 5.10.2006
70%	6.10.2006 – 5.10.2008
60%	6.10.2008 – 5.10.2010
50%	6.10.2010 or later

People who have evidence that they were clearly misinformed by the DWP and who are not fully covered by these proposals still have access to the usual procedures for dealing with maladministration in the Department (which can mean that an ex gratia payment is given).

Inherited S2P

A widow or widower will also be able to inherit their husband's or wife's S2P. However, this will be at the 50 per cent rate from the beginning.

Benefits under the rules before April 2001

The previous rules for widow's benefits still apply for a woman who lost her husband before 9 April 2001:

- If you had dependent children when your husband died, you may receive a Widowed Mother's Allowance, which lasts until the youngest child is 16 (or 19 if still in full-time education).
- If you did not have dependent children, but were between 55 and 64, you may receive a Widow's Pension, followed by a State Pension (see below).
- If you are aged over 55 when your Widowed Mother's Allowance runs out, you move on to the Widow's Pension at that point.
- If you are between 45 and 55 when either of these things happen, you receive a reduced 'age-related' widow's benefit.

Widowers were discriminated against under the old rules but, as explained above, those with dependent children have been able to start drawing the new Widowed Parent's Allowance from 9 April 2001, whenever it was they lost their partner. If you are making a claim now, however, it will not be backdated more than three months.

Choosing between Widow's Pension and State Pension

Widows receiving benefits under the old rules still have the choice of continuing to receive the Widow's Pension until their 65th birthday. The amounts will often be the same, but you may also receive some Graduated Pension with the State Pension. Ask for a pension forecast (see pages 61–63) six months or so before you reach 60 to check what is best.

Transitional help for older widows and widowers

People who were over 55 when the new benefits began in April 2001, and who lose their husband or wife within five years, are allowed to claim means-tested Income Support without being required to follow the normal rules about seeking a job. They are also entitled to a special bereavement premium on Income Support, once the Bereavement Allowance explained above ends, to bring it up to the same rate as the Bereavement Allowance.

For more information, see social security guide NP45 *A Guide to Bereavement Benefits* and leaflet GL14 *Widowed*?

PENSIONS AND DIVORCE

The rules explained below will also apply to the dissolution of Civil Partnerships after December 2005. The term 'divorce' is used here to cover both.

The State Basic Pension

There are some special rules which help divorced people who do not qualify for a full pension based on their own contributions, so long as they have not remarried. If you are in this position, you may be able to use your former spouse's contribution record to fill in gaps in your own and to help you qualify for a State Basic Pension. The Pension Service checks both contribution records when you retire. If your former spouse's record will give you a better pension than your own record, they substitute it for yours. They can do this either from the date of the marriage to the date of divorce or from the beginning of your 'working life' up to the date of divorce (or the year before State Pension age in both cases). This makes no difference to the former spouse – it is simply a book-keeping exercise.

Under the 'pension sharing' rules (explained on pages 158–160) it is possible for the SERPS/S2P pension to be divided as part of the divorce settlement, like any other pension. It is rare for judges to order this, however.

If you get divorced before State Pension age and have been paying contributions at the reduced (married woman's) rate, you will have to transfer to the full rate. If you are divorced after State Pension age and are receiving the married woman's pension, you may be able to use these rules to get a full pension. In this case, it is the husband's contribution record, up to the year in which you reach State Pension age, which counts.

If you remarry

If you remarry before State Pension age, you lose the right to use your former spouse's contribution record for your pension.

If you divorce again, you can use only the last spouse's contribution record in this way. However, if you remarry after State Pension age you do not lose the pension you already have.

For more information, see HMRC leaflet CA10 *National Insurance Contributions for Divorcees.*

Example

Joan is divorced after 30 years of marriage. She remarries at the age of 58 to a man five years younger than herself. She has not paid enough NI contributions for a pension in her own right, so she will get a pension only when her second husband qualifies for one at the age of 65.

However, if she had postponed the marriage until she was over 60, she might have been able to get a full Basic Pension based on her former husband's contribution record.

Separated people

Because the marriage is still legally in existence, the arrangements for spouses to make use of each other's contribution record do not apply. But when the husband in a separated couple claims his State Pension, his wife will be able to claim a married woman's pension of £49.15 if she does not qualify for a pension on her own NI record.

If a woman in a separated couple is under 60, her husband will get the dependant's increase for her if he is 'contributing to her maintenance' by paying at least the same rate as the increase (£49.15 in 2005–2006). The rules discriminate against men, however: for a woman to get an increase for her husband, she must in addition have been receiving incapacity pension with an increase for him as a dependant, before she went on to State Pension. From 2010 onwards, the rules will be the same for men and women.

DRAWING YOUR PENSION

About four months before you reach State Pension age you should be sent a retirement pack including an 'invitation to claim'. Put in your application as soon as possible after receiving the form, to make sure that you receive your first payment on time. If you have not received one three months before that date, you need to take action. It may be a simple slip-up, they may not have an up-to-date address for you, or it may mean that your age and contribution record have been wrongly recorded.

✱ Action Points

Phone the Pension Service on 0845 300 1084 (7am–7pm) for the Teleclaims Service, which allows you to begin making your claim by phone. Alternatively, you can download a form over the Internet (from www.thepensionservice.gov.uk), print it out and send it off.

A married woman claiming a pension on her husband's contributions needs to make a separate claim.

If you deferred your pension rather than starting to draw it when you reached State Pension age, in order to gain extra pension, as explained on pages 75–78, it is your responsibility to notify The Pension Service when you wish to start claiming your pension.

How your pension is paid

If you are starting your pension now, then it will normally be paid straight into your bank, building society or post office account. Depending on the account you use, you can take your money out at cash machines, branches of your bank or building society, the Post Office, and at the checkouts of supermarkets with a 'cashback' facility. New pensioners who do not want to be paid in this way will need to contact The Pension Service to discuss their options and it should then be possible for them to receive weekly cheques in the post.

For more information, see DWP leaflet DPL1 *Direct Payment: Giving It to You Straight*, or ring the DWP's Freephone helpline on the topic on 0800 107 2000.

Most pensions of £5 a week or less are paid once a year, in December, in arrears.

Pay-day for someone retiring now is usually Monday. You cannot receive any pension for days of retirement before your first pay-day, and the pension is only payable for whole weeks. This means, however, that it is not stopped until the end of the week in which the pensioner dies.

INCREASING YOUR PENSION

Making voluntary contributions

If you have had an interrupted career, and so would otherwise qualify for only a small Basic Pension in your own right, or you do not have enough qualifying years to get one at all, it may be worth paying voluntary contributions to increase your pension entitlement. For a married woman, whether this is worth doing or not will depend largely on whether you are older or younger than your husband. It is more likely to be worthwhile if you are the same age or older than your husband, as with changing from reduced-rate to full-rate contributions. However, voluntary contributions cannot be paid for years when you were paying contributions at the married woman's reduced rate (explained on pages 51–53).

Normally, voluntary contributions can be paid only for gaps within the last six years. However, HM Revenue & Customs has announced that anyone wishing to pay voluntary National Insurance contributions for the tax years 1996–1997 to 2000–2001 will now have extra time to do so. It has sent out around 10 million Deficiency Notices to people who had gaps in their contribution records over this time, and is extending the time limit for filling gaps which have occurred in its customers' National Insurance accounts between April 1996 and 5 April 2008. (In addition, the DWP has sent out notices to over half a million pensioners who could see an immediate increase in their pensions if they make retrospective contributions, at a cost to the Government of around £100m. They have until 2010 to make a claim.)

✳ Action Points

If you have had a 'Deficiency Notice' from HM Revenue & Customs about paying voluntary contributions, look at HMRC leaflet CA93 *Short Fall in your NICs: National Insurance Contributions: To Pay or Not to Pay?* before you make up your mind whether to do so or not. Also ask for a pension forecast (see pages 61–63). It may be that with credits and Home Responsibilities Protection you already have a sufficient contribution record for a full pension. If, however, you have a gap which can be made up by paying one or two years' extra contributions, it may well be worthwhile.

Deferring your pension

You can choose to defer drawing your pension and receive an increase in the weekly payment when you do start drawing it, or a taxable lump sum if you prefer.

Under the new rules from April 2005, if you defer your pension for at least five weeks it will be increased by one fifth of 1 per cent (0.2) for each week you defer – this works out as 1 per cent for each five weeks. Your pension will be increased by around 10.4 per cent for each full year that you do not draw it. For example, if you defer your pension for five years it will be increased by just over half. Your Additional and Graduated Pensions will be increased in the same way as the Basic Pension.

Alternatively, instead of an increased pension you could receive a one-off taxable lump-sum payment. This will be calculated based on the amount of pension you have forgone and a compounded interest rate of at least 2 per cent above the Bank of England base rate. You must put off claiming your State Pension for at least 12 consecutive months (which must be all after 5 April 2005) to have the choice of a lump-sum payment. You will not accrue an increased pension or lump-sum payment if you receive certain other benefits or another category of State Pension while you are deferring your pension.

If you do not put off drawing your pension for a full year, you can receive an increased pension (as long as you put off drawing it for at least five weeks) or you can receive your pension backdated to the time when you could have started to receive it (but without any interest payments).

Deferment for married women

If you are a married woman entitled to a State Pension on your own contributions and you defer drawing it, the pension will be increased (or you can take a one-off lump-sum payment) as described above.

If you are entitled to a State Pension (or an increase to your pension) based on your husband's contributions, you can only draw this when your husband claims his own pension. If he decides to defer claiming his pension you will not be able to draw any pension based on his contributions until he stops deferring his, but when you do draw it you will get an increase (or a lump sum).

However, you will not get an increase or a lump-sum payment for deferring the pension from your husband's contributions if, while your husband is deferring his pension, you draw any pension you are entitled to on your own contributions or certain other benefits. It may be better not to draw your own pension (for example, if this is a small amount) if your husband is deferring his pension.

If you die before drawing the pension

If you die before starting to draw the pension, leaving a surviving spouse (or civil partner after December 2005: see pages 39–40), he or she will be able to inherit at least part of the deferred pension or the lump sum, provided that:

- they were married (or registered as civil partner) to the deceased at the time of death;
- they have reached State Pension age (but see below for the position for younger people); and
- they have claimed their own State Pension, without having remarried before doing so.

If the surviving spouse/civil partner is below State Pension age when someone deferring their State Pension dies, the lump sum will be kept for them, increasing in line with prices, until the date when they claim their own State Pension.

The spouse/civil partner inherits different proportions of the deferred pension or lump sum, from different components of the State Pension. So they will get:

- 100 per cent of the increments or lump sum built up on the Basic State Pension;
- 50 per cent of those built up on S2P;
- 50 per cent of those built up on the Graduated Pension; and
- between 50 per cent and 100 per cent of those built up on their SERPS benefits, depending on the date at which their spouse/civil partner reached State Pension age (see page 68, for a table showing how these payments are being phased down).

Income Tax and the impact on income-related benefits

The State Pension is taxable and is taken into account for benefits such as Pension Credit, Housing Benefit and Council Tax Benefit. If you receive an increased pension following deferment this will count as part of your taxable income and may reduce the amount of any income-related benefits you receive. However, the lump-sum payment from April 2006 will be ignored if you claim Pension Credit, Housing Benefit or Council Tax Benefit. The lump sum will be taxed at the rate at which you are currently paying Income Tax (so will not put you into a different tax band). You can choose to delay receiving it until the following tax year, which may be an advantage if your income is lower then.

Is it worth deferring?

Given current life expectancy it is far more likely than not that someone who is in good health at State Pension age will still be going strong (barring accidents) five or six years later. Now that you can have the whole deferred pension paid as a lump sum, you only need last that long for your family to see the benefit. If you have a spouse who qualifies, then, as explained above, he or she can inherit a proportion of the pension or lump sum.

The alternative, if you do not need your State Pension yet, is to draw it and add it to your savings. Then at least there is an asset there whatever happens to you. You could pay part or all of it into a stakeholder pension and have the Income Tax added back by HM Revenue & Customs.

It is worth considering deferment, however, if drawing the State Pension would take you into a higher tax bracket (from 10 per cent to 22 per cent or from 22 per cent to 40 per cent), and you are not concerned about leaving money for others to inherit.

For more information, see DWP leaflet SPD1 *Your State Pension Choice: Pension Now or Extra Pension Later: A Guide to State Pension Deferral.*

✽ Action Points

Check whether your earnings will affect any income-related (means-tested) benefits you might be entitled to. You may find that you do not gain very much extra income by working.

If so, consider whether you might prefer to do voluntary work or pursue other interests. Make sure you have full information, and get advice if you are not sure about the different options.

MEANS-TESTED BENEFITS FOR PENSIONERS

As well as providing the State pensions paid for out of National Insurance contributions, the State provides a number of other benefits paid for our of our taxes, which are means-tested – in other words, whether you receive the benefit, and how much it is, depends on how much other income (and in some cases also capital) you have.

The main benefits of this sort are:

- Pension Credit
- Housing Benefit
- Council Tax Benefit

This section gives a very brief introduction to these three benefits. For further information, see the Age Concern publication *Your Rights* (see page 269).

Pension Credit

Pension Credit is a weekly social security entitlement for people aged 60 and over with low or modest incomes. You do not need to have paid National Insurance (NI) contributions to qualify for Pension Credit, but your income and any savings and capital over a certain level will be taken into account. Pension Credit is not taxable.

It has two parts – the guarantee credit and the savings credit. The guarantee credit helps with weekly basic living expenses by topping up your income to a level set by the Government. The savings credit provides additional cash to people aged 65 and over who have income over a certain level, from sources such as pensions and savings. It does not have an upper capital limit. People may be entitled to the guarantee credit or the savings credit or both.

If you receive Pension Credit and you are liable to pay rent and/or Council Tax, then you are also likely to qualify for Housing Benefit (HB) and/or Council Tax Benefit (CTB) to help with these bills. Even if your income is too high for you to receive Pension Credit, you may still be entitled to HB and CTB.

Pension Credit can be paid to homeowners, tenants, and people in other circumstances such as living with family or friends. You can work and receive Pension Credit, although most of your earnings will be taken into account. Once you get Pension Credit, you may also be able to apply for other benefits such as lump-sum payments from the Social Fund, while if you are entitled to the guarantee credit this will 'passport' you to help with health costs such as help towards glasses and free dental treatment.

For more information, see Age Concern Factsheet 48 *Pension Credit* and social security leaflet PC1L *Pension Credit: Pick It Up: It's Yours* or the more detailed social security guide PC10S.

✳ Action Points

If you are not sure whether you qualify, apply anyway. Alternatively, The Pension Service or a local advice agency may be able to give you an idea of any possible entitlement. If you have access to the Internet, you could look at the Pension Credit calculator on The Pension Service website (www.thepensionservice.gov.uk).

Remember that even if you are not entitled to Pension Credit when you first retire, as you get older and further away from retirement you will be steadily more likely to qualify. This is because the Pension Credit rates are expected to increase faster than your other pension income does. Also, you and/or your partner may become disabled as you get older. So even if you are turned down once, it will be worth applying again in a few years' time.

Housing Benefit and Council Tax Benefit

Housing Benefit (HB) provides help with rent, with certain service charges and, in Northern Ireland, with general rates.

Council Tax Benefit (CTB) is a social security benefit which provides help with paying the Council Tax. There are also other ways your Council Tax bill may be reduced, not related to your income or savings – see *Your Rights* for details (see page 269).

Second adult rebate

If you are solely liable to pay the Council Tax, you might get a second adult rebate if one or more people with a low income live with you, regardless of the level of your savings and income.

✳ Action Points

If you think you might qualify for one of these benefits, look at *Your Rights* for details, or ask your local council, advice agency or Age Concern for advice. If in doubt, claim. Once you are getting the benefit, you will also need to tell the local authority about relevant changes in your circumstances. They should tell you what these are, and how you should report them.

EARLY RETIREMENT AND STATE BENEFITS

It is not possible to draw the State Pension early in the UK. If you take early retirement from your job (whether voluntary or enforced), there are other State benefits you *may* be able to get, covering unemployment and sickness, and once you are 60 you can claim Pension Credit.

If you are thinking about whether to take early retirement for whatever reason, the safest assumption is that you will receive *nothing* from the National Insurance system (and you might have to pay contributions to it) until you reach State Pension age. Base your budget on your own resources. If this means that you will find it hard to survive, you may need to think again about retiring. Before age 60, means-tested Income Support will be available if you are badly off, but there is a large gap between what the State considers is enough to live on under Income Support, and what is necessary for a comfortable and enjoyable retirement. However, whether male or female, once you reach 60 you become entitled to the 'guarantee credit' element of Pension Credit, which is much more generous than Income Support for those under 60. If you have been struggling on because you did not feel you could afford to retire before, you might wish to look again at the position once you reach your 60th birthday.

Becoming too sick or disabled to work

The Government has announced that it plans to make major changes in the benefit arrangements described below, probably from 2008. According to this announcement, initially people will be put on a holding benefit paid at Jobseeker's Allowance rates, with access to the new reformed benefits only once they have been through a medical assessment. This will take place within 12 weeks, and be accompanied by a new Employment and Support Assessment. Two new benefits, called Rehabilitation Support Allowance and Disability and Sickness Allowance, will differentiate between those who have a severe condition and those with potentially more manageable conditions.

Those with more manageable conditions will receive the *Rehabilitation Support Allowance*. It will offer everyone a basic benefit at the same level as Jobseeker's Allowance (around £55 in today's terms) but then ensure that they can build up to get more than today's long-term Incapacity Benefit rate by giving them extra money, first for attending Work Focused Interviews, and then also for taking steps to get them back towards the labour market. Those with the most severe conditions will receive more money than now on the *Disability and Sickness Allowance*. They will be able to volunteer to take up employment support.

There will be consultations before the changes are brought in, and existing claimants will be safeguarded, although they may also be able to make use of the offers of help in getting back into the labour market.

Incapacity Benefit

Currently, people in employment are usually covered by Statutory Sick Pay (SSP) for the first 28 weeks that they are too sick or disabled to work. After that, Incapacity Benefit (IB) is paid at the rate of £68.20 up to the 52nd week, and then at £76.45 for as long as you qualify. There is some additional money for those who become sick or disabled below the age of 45. There are limited additions for spouses, while children are covered by the Child Tax Credit.

People not entitled to SSP, for example because they are self-employed or out of work, and who become incapable of work, may get a lower rate of Incapacity Benefit (£57.65 a week) for the first 28 weeks. This is not taxable. For other claimants, except those already on the old Invalidity Benefit when the rules changed in April 1995, the benefit is taxable.

Once you reach State Pension age (currently, 60 for women, 65 for men) you transfer over automatically to the State Pension.

If you go abroad to live, you retain your right to Incapacity Benefit if you are moving within the European Union, but the benefit can be denied if you move elsewhere, even if you fulfil the contribution conditions.

The test for Incapacity Benefit

The test of whether you are 'incapacitated', after the 28-week period, is called the 'Personal Capability Assessment'. The criteria are not related to what job you could realistically find, but to your ability to perform certain functions relevant to work. These include, for example, sitting, standing, walking, lifting, manual handling, speech, comprehension and behaviour. A score is given for each of these, on a scale of severity. You receive benefits only if you score sufficiently highly on one or several of these.

Some groups do not have to undergo the medical test:

- people who receive the highest rate of the care component of Disability Living Allowance; and

- people with certain chronic or severe conditions (a detailed list of these is included in DWP leaflet IB214).

(There are also some special rules for people who were receiving Invalidity Benefit on 13 April 1995 when the scheme changed.)

You may be told that you are not sick enough to qualify for Incapacity Benefit although you or your employer consider that you are too sick for work. Ask for advice from a Citizens Advice Bureau or other advice agency. Many people who are turned down for Incapacity Benefit appeal to an independent Social Security Appeal Tribunal, and find that they are then granted the benefit.

National Insurance contribution requirements

As well as the medical tests, there are rules about the number of National Insurance contributions you must have paid:

- at some point in your working life, you must have actually *paid* contributions, on earnings of at least 25 times the Lower Earnings Limit (explained on page 47) for that year, in one tax year out of the last three years in the calendar year before you make your claim (but see page 47 if your earnings are between the LEL and the Earnings Threshold); and
- within the last two tax years before the calendar year in which you make your claim, you must have either paid or been credited with contributions on earnings of at least 50 times the Lower Earnings Limit in those years.

The main effect of this (and the idea behind it) is that if you have been unemployed or early retired for a time before you fall ill, you may not be able to claim Incapacity Benefit whatever the medical test says.

Occupational and personal pensions and Incapacity Benefit

If you have been on Incapacity Benefit since before April 2001, and you continue to qualify, it will be paid in full no matter what your other income. For new IB claims after that date, however, if you have more than £85 a week of occupational pension, personal pension, or Permanent Health Insurance (PHI) payment provided by your employer, your IB will be reduced by 50p for every £1 of your pension income above this limit. However, you avoid this deduction if the PHI is paid through your employer's payroll (as it usually is). Your benefit will not be reduced if you receive the highest rate of the care component of Disability Living Allowance.

For more information, see social security leaflet SD3 *Long-Term Ill or Disabled?*

Example

Adriana has had to take early retirement because of stress and has an occupational pension of £115 a week. To find out what IB she will lose:

deduct £85, leaving £30

divide £30 by 2 = £15

So she will lose £15 of her IB.

Jobseeker's Allowance

If you have taken early retirement but do not qualify for IB, you may be able to claim contribution-based Jobseeker's Allowance (JSA) for up to 26 weeks, provided that you have paid sufficient NI contributions. To qualify you must be unemployed and actively seeking work.

You may be disqualified from JSA for up to 26 weeks if you leave a job voluntarily 'without just cause'. If you have chosen to accept early retirement, you may therefore be disqualified from benefit. If this happens, seek advice from a Citizens Advice Bureau or other advice agency.

Jobseeker's Allowance comes in two forms – contribution-based and income-based. Contribution-based JSA is paid for up to six months, if you qualify because you have made the right National Insurance contributions. However, it is only paid for you as an individual, not for your spouse or family, and it is only £56.20 a week (for those aged 25 or over) in 2005–2006. Income-based JSA is intended to provide money for them from the start, and for you once the six months are up. As the name suggests, it is means-tested – in other words, both your income and your capital are taken into account in deciding whether you qualify.

If you receive an occupational or personal pension, contribution-based JSA will be reduced by the amount your pension exceeds £50.

If you have capital of more than £8,000 (£12,000 if you or your partner are aged 60 or over), you will not be entitled to claim income-based JSA (even if your weekly income is low), so then you will receive contribution-based JSA for six months only and no State benefits thereafter, although you may well qualify for Housing Benefit or Council Tax Benefit.

If your spouse or partner works 24 hours a week or more, there will be no entitlement for either of you to income-based JSA (although you might be eligible for Working Tax Credit).

You also have to show that you are 'actively seeking work'. All claimants have to sign a Jobseeker's Agreement, committing them to take certain steps to find a job. You claim JSA from your local

Jobcentre Plus office, where you will be given a claim pack and an interview will be arranged.

In the past, in general Jobcentres did not try particularly hard to help (or pressure) people over 50 to find new jobs if they were unemployed. However, it has been announced that the DWP now has a 'public service target' for increasing the employment rate of people aged between 50 and 69, between Spring 2005 and Spring 2008. The DWP, Jobcentre Plus and The Pension Service will work to ensure that individuals know of available opportunities.

Redundancy pay

There are statutory minimum figures for redundancy payments, but you may find that your employer offers a better package. Some elements of these payments, such as money in lieu of notice, can prevent you receiving JSA for the weeks they are expected to cover. Get advice from the Citizens Advice Bureau or your trade union if you have been affected in this way or if you feel your redundancy pay has been wrongly calculated.

Where an employee is within 12 months of his or her 65th birthday, the statutory redundancy entitlement is reduced by one-twelfth for each complete month after the 64th birthday. This 'tapering' gradually reduces entitlement to nothing by the time the employee reaches the age of 65.

If you are within 90 weeks of the retirement age set by your employer, it is legally allowable for redundancy pay to be reduced or even lost altogether by 'offsetting' it against the value of the pension rights. Good employers rarely do this, however, except perhaps as part of a more generous early retirement package. Older employees who suspect that they may be made redundant should check in advance whether this offsetting will apply. You must be notified if this is to be applied to you.

For more information, see Department of Trade and Industry leaflet PL808 *Redundancy Entitlement Statutory Rights: A Guide for Employees.* Copies are available on the DTI website at www.dti.gov.uk/publications

Protecting your State Pension in early retirement

If you are planning to retire early, check whether you have paid enough NI contributions to receive a full Basic Pension when you reach State Pension age. You can do this by getting a pension forecast, as explained on pages 61–63.

You will receive NI credits towards your pension if you are drawing a benefit such as Jobseeker's Allowance or Incapacity Benefit. If you are under 60 and seeking work, it could well be worth registering for Jobseeker's Allowance – even if you are not entitled to benefit – in order to receive credits. If you are a man aged 60–64, you will automatically receive credits even though you are not signing on as unemployed or receiving another benefit, as long as you are not self-employed or abroad for more than half the year.

If you are not entitled to credits and have an incomplete NI record, you may want to consider paying Class 3 voluntary contributions (see pages 74–75).

WORKING AFTER STATE PENSION AGE

Once you have reached State Pension age (currently 60 for women, 65 for men), and provided you satisfy the contribution conditions, you can draw your State Pension. If you decide to carry on working or to take another job, your State Pension will not be affected by the amount you earn or the number of hours you work.

You will be liable to pay Income Tax on your pension and your earnings (your tax code will be adjusted to take into account any pension you receive), but you will not have to pay NI contributions. You should receive a certificate of exception from the DWP to give to your employer. Your employer will still have to pay its share of NI contributions for you.

NON-STATE PENSIONS: THE DIFFERENT TYPES AND FRAMEWORKS

Alongside the State Pensions explained in the last chapter, there is a whole array of different sorts of non-State pensions. Given the low level of State benefits, anyone who wants a comfortable retirement will need to have one (or more) of these, unless they have money invested in other things.

This chapter covers the different ways in which pensions offered by bodies other than the State can build up (defined benefit or defined contribution); the different legal categories of pension (statutory, trust-based or contract-based); and the ways in which each type of pension can be either contracted out of S2P/SERPS (replacing it), or contracted in (on top of it). Finally, it also covers the current rules about giving tax relief for pensions, and the new ones which come in after April 2006.

THE WAYS IN WHICH PENSIONS BUILD UP

There are two main ways in which non-State pensions can build up (with some complex 'hybrids' between the different types), and the first type is broken down into three different sub-groups.

Using the US names, which are now becoming standard in the UK, the main types are:

- **Defined benefit**, where there is a commitment to pay a pension calculated through a certain formula linked in one way or another to earnings; and
- **Defined contribution**, where the commitment or arrangement is about how much money goes in as a contribution, and there is no entitlement to a particular level of pension. What matters is how well it is invested, and how the resulting 'pot' of money is handled at the time of retirement. The older UK name for this sort of pension is 'money-purchase'.

For most members of defined-benefit schemes, the commitment is to a pension linked to their earnings at or close to retirement. These are generally called 'final-salary schemes' and are explained in more detail below. There are also two other types which are growing in popularity among employers:

- **Career-average salary schemes**, where the pension is linked to earnings throughout your life with that employer, revalued by some formula (explained on pages 95–97); and
- **Cash-balance schemes** (another US import), where you build up a proportion of your salary as a notional account within the pension scheme. This is increased each year according to a set formula, and at retirement you have a 'pot' of money with which you can buy a pension at the going rate. (These are explained on pages 97–98.)

DEFINED-BENEFIT SCHEMES

These schemes all involve a commitment to a certain level of benefit. This means that if the investment returns are not enough to produce that level, contributions have to be increased to pay for the benefit if the scheme is to survive. For this reason, there must be an employer or a group of employers standing behind the scheme. So all defined-benefit schemes are occupational, whether statutory or trust-based.

Final-salary schemes

These are the most common type of defined-benefit scheme. To work out the pension, four definitions in the scheme rules are important:

- Pensionable salary
- *Final* pensionable salary
- Pensionable service
- The 'accrual rate' (the rate at which the pension builds up each year).

Different schemes use different names for the same thing, so the first item for example might be 'scheme salary', 'pensionable earnings', 'pensionable pay' or any one of many other names. The last item, the accrual rate, will usually be a fraction (such as 1/60th) or a percentage (such as 1.5 per cent).

Having got these figures, to work out the pension, the formula is:

- Take final pensionable salary;
- Multiply by the accrual rate (for example, by $\frac{1}{60}$); and
- Multiply by number of years in scheme (often called 'pensionable service').

In the simplest scheme, pensionable salary is the same as your gross salary, and final pensionable salary would be your pensionable salary in the last 12 months before you retire. The most common accrual rate is 1/60th, and most schemes say that pensionable service is simply the years and complete months you have worked for that employer since you joined the scheme.

Example

Jane joined the ABC company scheme at 20, and is now due to retire at 60, so she has exactly 40 years' pensionable service. Her gross pay, in the last year before retirement, is £24,000 a year. So: £24,000 multiplied $\frac{1}{60}$ (the accrual rate = £400. £400 x 40 = £16,000.

Schemes like this give employees some certainty. Currently, with inflation so low, a pension like this is an inflation-proofed investment whether she stays in the scheme or leaves – although if inflation rises above 5 per cent, there will be a ceiling on the inflation-proofing for those in the private (but not the public) sector.

The pension in these schemes is based on earnings at retirement or on leaving the scheme, not on the earnings when the contributions went into the scheme. Someone in their 40s or 50s may have seen their earnings multiply by 20 or 30 times during their working lives. Prices have gone up vastly also, but most people's earnings – and so also their final-salary pensions – have kept pace with prices or increased faster.

However, providing good and reliable benefits to scheme members is expensive, and the employer is carrying a substantial risk. During the 1980s and much of the 1990s things were going very well for occupational pension schemes, and they were very cheap to run. Now that investment returns are down and the actuaries are predicting greater life expectancy, things are not going so well. Employers are becoming increasingly reluctant to provide final-salary schemes, and many existing ones are being closed to new starters. Many pension schemes now have too little money in them to cover the promises that have been made. If the employer closes them down, there may be a gap. In general, employers who already have schemes are changing the design, rather than abandoning pensions altogether.

Career-average salary schemes

These are also salary-related, but in this case they take the pensionable salary for each year you have been in the scheme, and average it out to give a final figure. Because of inflation, the earnings figures in the past now look very low compared with today's figures, so before doing this averaging they generally *revalue* these figures to take account of the way either earnings or prices (depending on how good the scheme is) have risen generally in the meantime. There may also be a ceiling on the level of revaluation, so that if inflation rises the revaluation will not keep up fully.

These schemes are rare, but Tesco, Nationwide and Sainsbury's all have them, with guaranteed revaluation limited to prices (but with options for the trustees to provide additional increases). Two of the big public-sector arrangements, the NHS and the Civil Service, may move over from final-salary to career-average over the next few years, although the pension that has already built up is likely to be protected. Here is an example (taken from the Cabinet Office consultation document) of how a new career-average Civil Service scheme might work.

"We will call the proportion of pay used to calculate each year's pension the *retirement savings factor* and express this as a percentage. The retirement savings factor will be multiplied by pensionable earnings each year to give the amount of pension earned for that year. The amount of pension earned for each year will increase in line with retail prices... regardless of whether the member is in service, has left with a deferred or 'frozen' pension, or has already drawn their pension...

Example

Ella joins the scheme on 1 May 2005. In the period to 31 March 2007 Ella earns £16,000.

On the assumption that the pension scheme had a retirement savings factor of 2 per cent*, these earnings would give Ella an index-linked pension of £320 a year, payable at age 65.

In the following year to 31 March 2008, Ella earns £18,000. These earnings would give her a further pension of £360 a year, so that her total index-linked pension is now £680 a year.

Ella's pension will continue to increase in this way, reflecting her earnings in each and every year of service. Ella's pension will also increase in line with prices, both before she draws it and during her retirement."

*The 2 per cent figure is higher than the 1.67 per cent (1/60th) accrual rate currently used in the equivalent Civil Service scheme because over time, earnings tend to increase faster than prices, so a higher factor is needed to provide an equivalent pension. The consultation document stresses that this figure is for 'illustrative purposes' only, and the actual figure may be different when the new Civil Service scheme is finalised.

(Source: *Civil Service Pensions: Building a Sustainable Future*, Cabinet Office, 2004)

A good career-average scheme can benefit people who are on flat pay rates, or whose earnings fluctuate during their working lives – including many women, who may have long periods of part-time work. It is also likely to give more predictable costs to the employer. Those it does not benefit compared with a good final-salary scheme, however, are people who get good promotions late in their careers, and those on incremental scales. These are people whose best earnings in *real* terms (in other words, in terms of the standard of living it gives them) are at the end of their working lives, so having the pension calculated on the basis of this final salary is of benefit. So if an employer is trying to change between the different types, it can be very divisive between the various groups of staff.

Cash-balance schemes

In these schemes, each member's benefit builds up in an individual 'pot', which is used to buy an annuity at retirement. The value of each 'pot' is expressed as a cash balance or lump sum. It builds up cumulatively, with an accrual rate calculated as a percentage of pensionable earnings each year.

The pensionable earnings figure may be based on the member's final earnings at retirement, or it may be based on current earnings but with extra bonuses added by the trustees depending on investment conditions. Members may have the opportunity to put in different levels of contributions and so build up different percentages. There may also be an element of revaluation built into the scheme's design, to take account of inflation.

Cash-balance schemes give more predictable costs for the employers, but with the investment risk staying with them rather than being passed to the employees as in defined-contribution schemes. However, when the member reaches retirement they will need to buy an annuity with the 'pot' of money, and so they are vulnerable to changes in this market and the likelihood that annuities will become more expensive as a result of increased life expectancy. Some cash-balance schemes provide specially tailored annuities for their members, which means they do not see some of their funds disappearing in profits to insurance companies.

These schemes are very unusual in the UK, but much more common in the USA. One UK example is the department store chain House of Fraser. It has a two-tier scheme, where either 10 per cent or 20 per cent of salary is credited to the member's 'account' each year. The money in the account built up so far is increased in line with the Retail Prices Index, to a maximum of 5 per cent.

DEFINED-CONTRIBUTION (MONEY-PURCHASE) SCHEMES

The other type of pension scheme, the defined-contribution (DC) or money-purchase scheme, works in very much the same way as any other private investment. Because these schemes don't carry a promise of a particular level of pension, they do not need an employer to stand behind them. There are, however, many trust-based occupational schemes which are DC (although none of the statutory ones). All personal and stakeholder pensions, and most of the AVC arrangements that are provided alongside occupational schemes, are DC.

This means that contributions, and the investment returns on them, go into an individual 'pot' which is then used for the pension. There will often be a choice of different investment funds into which to put your contributions (and the employer's, if there are any) – some more, some less risky. Many schemes offer also a 'default' option, where your money is put if you do not make a choice yourself. This may be what is called a 'lifestyle' or 'lifecycle' fund, which means that it is invested to start with in company shares (which can be risky but have at least in the past tended to do better in the long run) and is then moved into safer but lower-return investments such as gilts (lending money to the Government) as you come up to retirement.

At retirement, part of the 'pot' is paid out in a tax-free lump sum, and the rest goes to buy an annuity (see pages 237–244).

DC pensions have been around for a very long time, but their numbers have grown in recent years. In particular, a number of employers, including some very large ones, have said recently that new starters cannot join their final-earnings scheme, but must go into a DC arrangement instead.

Your retirement income with a DC pension will depend on:

- the length of time the money has been invested;
- how good the investment returns were;
- how much you paid in management and commission charges;
- annuity rates when you start to draw the pension; and
- what type of annuity you choose.

This means that what one person gets from a DC pension can be very different from what their colleague gets, even if they have contributed the same amount over the same period of time. One key issue is the age at which you start making contributions. The further off from retirement you are, the more time your money has to build up investment returns and interest payments.

Example

Bill and **Mary** both start paying into a money-purchase scheme at the same time. Bill is 20 and Mary is 40. Their pension scheme achieves an average annual rate of return of 5 per cent. The table below shows how their original investment grows (in rounded figures) over the decades, up to the time they reach 60 and retire.

Age	Bill £	Mary £
20	1,000	
30	1,600	
40	2,700	1,000
50	4,300	1,600
60	7,100	2,700

You can find a more detailed calculation that shows this effect on the FSA website (www.fsa.gov.uk/consumer). This allows you to play around and see what the effect of putting in more at different ages would be. Remember, though, that these are only estimates, based on different levels of investment return that you might get.

THE LEGAL FRAMEWORKS

The second way of categorising non-State pensions is by how they are set up legally. Broadly – although with some hybrids again – there are three categories here:

- **Statutory** – with rules laid down by Acts of Parliament and Regulations. This applies to *most* schemes in the public sector, such as for the NHS and the Civil Service, although not all.

- **Trust-based** – with a Trust Deed setting out the framework, and trustees looking after the scheme. Organised collectively, schemes cover employees of one employer, a group of employers, or people within a particular employment sector, rather than people each having an individual contract.
- **Contract-based** – where the employer may also have a part in making the arrangements for the contracts, and may make a contribution towards each person's pension, but each individual who belongs has a contract or a policy document with the pension provider (generally an insurance company).

The first two types, statutory and trust-based, are generally called 'occupational pensions'. The third, contract-based, is the way that personal pensions, most stakeholder pensions, and all Free-Standing Additional Voluntary Contribution (FSAVC) arrangements are set up. (All these are explained in later sections.) If the employer takes a hand in arranging the personal or stakeholder pension and makes a contribution towards it, they are commonly called 'Group Personal' or 'Group Stakeholder' schemes.

Until April 2006, HM Revenue & Customs (formerly the Inland Revenue) is restricting the ways in which you can have pensions from more than one category, so that if you are a member of an employer's pension scheme – whether statutory or trust-based – you can only put a limited amount into a personal or stakeholder pension as well. After that date, however, the rules are being relaxed, so that you will have much more opportunity to 'pick and mix' between the different categories. There will still be maximum allowances for the amount you can put in as contributions and receive as pension while still getting tax relief, but these will be so much more generous than the current ones that for the vast majority of people they will be well above what they can afford anyway. The tax rules as they affect most people

are covered on pages 120–136. The special transitional rules for the higher-paid are explained on pages 133–134, but anyone who thinks they might be affected by the new limits should consult an accountant or financial adviser before April 2006.

STATUTORY SCHEMES

These are the occupational schemes set up by the Government to look after its own staff and those of other public services – the Civil Service, teaching, the NHS, and so on. At the moment all of them are defined-benefit (mostly final-salary) schemes, although the Treasury has floated the idea of having defined-contribution schemes as well.

Around 4 million people belong to these schemes, two-thirds of them women. Each scheme has a set of regulations (often voluminous) which set out the rules that have to be followed. Most of the statutory schemes are run by agencies, often with private contractors involved, on behalf of the Government. For example, the Teachers' Pension Agency runs the pension scheme for teachers in England and Wales, but all its work is contracted out to a private company called Capita (the same company that collects the London congestion charge, although a different division). Capita is only there to do the administration, however. It does not make the rules – that is the responsibility of the Department for Education and Skills (DfES), which tells Capita when to change its computer programs in line with changes in the regulations.

Most of these big public sector schemes are 'unfunded'. That means that when, for example, a teacher contributes 6 per cent of her salary towards her pension, it is not set aside as it would be in a private sector pension scheme. Instead, it goes into the overall Treasury coffers, and the pensions are also paid out of these coffers. The exception here is the Local Government Pension Scheme (LGPS) which is run by 99 different local authorities on behalf of the rest (and all following the same rules). Each pension authority has separate funds, adding up to around £80 billion in total.

This might all sound a bit insecure, but in fact statutory schemes are more secure than others, because they have the Government or local government standing behind them. In local government, for example, there is a legal requirement that the LGPS pensions are paid. If the County Treasurer were to run off with all the funds – not something that has ever happened – the council taxpayers would simply have to make up the difference.

For this reason, statutory schemes are not covered by the same rules about solvency as private sector trust-based schemes, and do not pay into the Pension Protection Fund (explained on pages 197–198), because there simply is not the need.

Some people who do not work directly for the public sector may also be in statutory schemes, or have a statutory element in their pensions. For example:

- Teachers in many independent schools have a right to belong to the Teachers' Pension Scheme.
- If you work for a firm which has a contract with the local council, perhaps to do refuse collection or run the payroll, you may be eligible to join the LGPS under what are called 'admitted body' rules. One big advantage of this is that if the contract changes hands in a few years' time, or is taken back in-house, you can stay in the same pension scheme.
- Some of the old nationalised industries that were privatised in the 1980s and 1990s have special statutory rules and provisions, protecting those who were employees at the time of privatisation. The two main examples here are the railways and the coal industry, but there is also some protection in other industries such

as electricity. Just how strong it is varies widely, but it can be very valuable. Your trade union is probably best placed to tell you about it.

TRUST-BASED OCCUPATIONAL SCHEMES

These are set up by private sector employers, or groups of employers, and by a few public sector employers. In many cases insurance companies, financial firms, or specialist firms like Capita will do all the administration, but they are not responsible for setting the rules. These schemes can be any of the types of defined-benefit scheme explained above, or defined contribution.

Because pension schemes are set up under trust, the money is held separately from the company's accounts, so it cannot be taken by creditors if the company goes into liquidation, unless there is a surplus after all the members have had their entitlement.

Almost anybody can be a trustee of a pension fund – including companies (corporate trustees). Many pension schemes allow some of the trustees to be selected by a ballot of the members, or appointed through the trade unions. There is a requirement that at least one-third of the trustees should be member-nominated, unless the employer or the trustees have persuaded the scheme members not to object to their opting out of this rule. Under *The Pensions Act 2004*, the rules will be tightened in due course so that every scheme must have at least one-third of their trustees nominated by a process which involves at least all the active members and pensioners of the scheme, and selected by some or all of the members. (Members with deferred pensions can be left out of the process.) The duties of trustees are to act fairly and honestly, with reasonable care and in good faith. Scheme members have a right to know who the trustees of their own fund are and to see the trust deed.

Most pension schemes have to produce an annual report and audited accounts, and all scheme members have a right to see these. Independent auditors have to check the accounts of the pension fund.

Most people who take on the job of being trustees are very conscientious, but there has not actually been a requirement on them to understand what they are doing until recently. Under *The Pensions Act 2004*, there are new rules aimed at ensuring that they do have 'knowledge and understanding' of pensions matters and of their own scheme. The Pensions Regulator (explained on pages 200–201) has produced checklists of what trustees should know, and there is to be an optional exam for them. The new rules come fully into effect in April 2006, but trustees should be gearing up for them before then.

The idea of having a trust is that your contributions, and the employer's contributions, are set aside and invested so that the money is there to provide a pension when you retire. With a DB scheme, there is a single 'pot' of money that builds up for this purpose. It can be very large – for example the Universities Superannuation Scheme, the scheme for university teaching staff, has a fund worth around £20bn. With DC schemes, each member has their own separate account, but it is still looked after by the trustees.

In a DB scheme, you have the promise of a pension and it is the trustees' job to see it is delivered. It's not entirely secure, however, because if the company became insolvent, there would be no employer to back up the promises. In recent years quite a number of people have lost their pensions in this way. So the Government has now brought in the Pension Protection Fund (explained on pages 197–198) to safeguard them, and has also tightened up the rules on what employers must pay. This does not give a full guarantee, but it has certainly improved on the position.

However, because of this a lot of employers have become reluctant to run trust-based schemes, feeling that the risk for them is too high. Instead they are arranging contract-based pensions for their employees, as explained in the next section.

CONTRACT-BASED PENSION ARRANGEMENTS

People often call these 'private' pensions. Their proper name, however, will generally be either 'personal' or 'stakeholder' pensions. You can also have an extra, contract-based pension arrangement on top of your occupational scheme, called a Free-Standing Additional Contribution Scheme (FSAVC) (explained on page 164), although these have never been very popular. Stakeholder pensions are a sub-group of personal pensions with special rules, as explained on pages 216–220. (To confuse matters further, a few stakeholder schemes are in fact trust-based rather than contract-based: this makes no difference to the way these schemes are run as far as the consumer is concerned, however.)

If you have a personal or stakeholder pension, you should have a set of policy documents, which are your contract with the provider. Make sure you hold onto these, as you will need them for claiming the pension in due course. The contract is between you and the provider. Even if it is a Group Personal Pension (GPP) scheme (see pages 212–213) with the employer taking a great deal of interest, the employer is not legally party to the contract. Because of this, all contract-based schemes are DC rather than DB. You *might* have a guarantee of a certain level of investment return from the provider, although these are increasingly rare and generally minimal. Your employer may also be making advice available to help you 'target' the right level of retirement provision, but that will be as far as it goes.

This means that the level of your DC benefit is pretty uncertain, but the chances of a contract-based pension scheme failing to pay out, whatever happens to your employer, are remote. It is very rare for an insurance company to go into liquidation, but holders of personal pension policies would normally be covered by the Financial Services Compensation Scheme (address on page 262) if this happened. Financial advisers and other providers are also generally covered by compensation schemes. In most cases, however, there are upper limits on what can be paid out, so it still pays to take care over selecting your policy.

CONTRACTED IN OR OUT OF S2P?

All the different types of pension considered so far can be contracted in or out of the State Second Pension (S2P, and previously SERPS). Broadly, the question is whether you receive your non-State pension instead of S2P or in addition to it. If it is the former, part of your National Insurance contributions, and those of the employer, are diverted into the non-State pension, but the way this is done, and what it means for the individual, varies. The idea behind each method is that you get a lower amount of pension from the State, and more from your non-State package, but there is no guarantee of this.

There are three contracting-out methods:

- the contracted-out salary-related (COSR) method, which is intended for DB schemes, mostly final salary;
- the contracted-out money-purchase (COMP) method, which is intended for occupational DC schemes; and
- the appropriate personal pension (APP) method, which is intended – not surprisingly – for personal and stakeholder schemes.

There are, however, some final-salary schemes contracted out by the COMP method, and also some occupational DC schemes contracted out by the COSR method. Most occupational DC schemes are not contracted out at all, for reasons explained on pages 111–112. Individuals in these schemes can contract themselves out if they wish through the APP method.

CONTRACTED-OUT SALARY-RELATED (COSR) SCHEMES

Most members of DB occupational pension schemes are contracted out of S2P by this method. This means that both you and your employer pay lower National Insurance contributions. The difference is called the 'rebate', and is currently 1.6 per cent of 'band earnings' (explained on page 56) for the employee. For the employer, it is 3.5 per cent of the same band of earnings.

The fact that you are getting this rebate will probably not show up on your pay slip, which will simply give the net NI figure. However, it means that someone who is earning, for example, £20,000 saves around £230 a year on their NI, while the employer saves more than twice that. There's no legal requirement that this money must go into the pension scheme, but it is assumed that at least as much will be going in there in order to provide the promised pension.

What a contracted-out scheme must provide

To be allowed to contract out of S2P (and previously SERPS), the scheme must meet some minimum standards, but these have changed over time.

Pension built up before 1997

In a COSR up until April 1997 the law said that the occupational pension built up must not be less than a Guaranteed Minimum Pension (GMP), which is roughly the same as you would have had if you had remained in SERPS. This had to override the normal scheme rules.

Example

Tony's pension scheme was contracted out, and the normal scheme rules said that only basic pay was pensionable. But Tony did a lot of shiftwork, and under the rules the Guaranteed Minimum Pension (GMP) was calculated taking account of this as well. So when Tony came up to retirement, the scheme administrator did two sets of calculations, on the normal rules and the GMP rules. Since the GMP was higher, this was what Tony received.

The GMP was worked out in a different way from SERPS, but to ensure that no one lost out, the National Insurance system made up any shortfall (so long as the scheme was sufficiently funded to meet the GMP requirement). As a result, many people, even if they have been contracted out since SERPS started in 1978, have a little bit of SERPS pension to come when they retire.

The original arrangement in 1978 was that, once the GMP started to be paid, the occupational scheme did not have to increase it at all; the State would do that through giving an increase in the State Pension. In 1986 this changed, and the employer became responsible for paying the first 3 per cent increase (depending on the rate of inflation) and the State paid the rest.

The original 'guarantees' given in 1978 about contracting out have unfortunately turned out not to be as solid as expected. In particular, should you have the bad luck to belong to a scheme that is wound up with a deficit, and is taken into the Pension Protection Fund (see pages 197–198), the GMP is not treated separately but is included in the overall figure for which you receive compensation. In calculating the pension due from the State, however, you are still treated as receiving the full GMP. The reason for this, the Government says, is that you have saved money in the past through the NI rebate, and so should not be treated the same as a person who has paid the full level of contributions.

Spouses' and partners' pensions

COSR schemes also have to pay widows' and widowers' GMPs, but there is not full equality here. Widows' GMPs have existed since the system started in 1978, and so they are half the member's GMP built up since 1978. Widowers' GMPs, however, only began in 1988, so they are only half the member's GMP built up since 1988 and so can only be based on nine years' contributions at most. In both cases, the widow's or widower's GMP need only be paid if the spouse is aged over 45, or has dependent children (in other words, they would have become entitled to Bereavement Allowance or Widowed Parent's Allowance if widowed before 9 April 2001 – see pages 65–66). In practice, many schemes are rather more generous and pay them at any age. Unless the widow or widower cohabits with a partner of the opposite sex or remarries before State Pension age, however, the widow's or widower's GMP must continue in payment for life – unlike Bereavement Allowance, for example, which is only payable for a maximum of 52 weeks.

Once the *Civil Partnerships Act* (explained on pages 39–40) is in force, COSR schemes will also be required to provide survivor pensions for civil partners, based on the member's service back to 1988. This will duplicate the position for widowers, but will pay less than for widows, whose rights go back to the start of contracting out in 1978. There is no requirement to pay anything to unmarried or unregistered partners.

Changes in April 1997

The rules above changed in 1997. For service after that, the scheme must be certified to be of the same standard as or better than a 'reference scheme' for at least 90 per cent of the membership. The idea is that most people will not lose out on pension compared with the position in SERPS.

Employers' schemes now have to provide limited inflation-proofing on pensions – both in payment and while they are deferred – on their own instead of sharing responsibility with the State. Until April 2005, if inflation went above 5 per cent a year, they needed to provide only a maximum of 5 per cent. This ceiling has now been reduced to 2.5 per cent for future service from 6 April 2005. This means that people in contracted-out schemes may end up with worse benefits than if they had remained in SERPS/S2P, and the risk of inflation above a modest level is carried by the employees and pensioners. It is not compulsory, however, to make the reduction from 5 per cent to 2.5 per cent, and many schemes will remain unchanged. Statutory (public sector) pension schemes do not have this ceiling, but give full inflation-proofing whatever the level of increase.

CONTRACTED-OUT MONEY-PURCHASE (COMP) SCHEMES

There are not many of these about, with only a few hundred thousand people contracted out by this route altogether. The rebate for contracting out of S2P via this route is age-related. This means that the older you are (up to the age of 50), the more money is paid from the National Insurance Fund into the scheme for your pension.

This works in a complicated way; each time the employer pays you, it will pay the full rebate from *your* NI contributions (1.6 per cent of your earnings between the lower and upper limits) into the pension scheme. But it will pay a rebate of only 1 per cent from *its* NI contributions into the scheme. HM Revenue & Customs will then check your age and pay over the rest of what is due (up to an additional 7.9 per cent in 2005–2006 for someone aged 55 or over) on 5 April 2006.

The reason for this is that the rebate is intended to cover the costs of the part of S2P you are foregoing. However, as we saw in the example on page 100, the closer to retirement you are, the less time your money has to build up investment returns, and so it buys less pension; or to put it the other way round, the *more* money you need to buy a given level of pension equivalent to the amount foregone in S2P.

Most providers say that the rebate is not enough to ensure that contracting out is value for money, and that is the main reason that COMP schemes are rare. It is much more common now to have a contracted-in money-purchase scheme (sometimes called a CIMP) and to let individuals contract themselves out if they want, through an APP (see below). As explained on page 118, many people are being advised not to contract out in this way.

Protected Rights

The minimum requirement in a COMP is that the National Insurance rebate must be invested to create a Protected Rights fund for each individual. When you retire, this must be used to buy an annuity, which from April 2005 can be flat-rate or index-linked. The annuity rate used to work out how much pension your pot of money can buy must also be equal for men and women. The Protected Rights fund cannot be paid out as a lump sum, although from 6 April 2006 this will be possible.

The rules have changed twice, in 1997 and 2002, but, broadly, when your Additional Pension entitlement is being calculated, you are assumed to be getting as much from your COMP as you would have had from SERPS/S2P for those years, so your State Additional Pension is reduced to take account of this.

If a member dies in service leaving a widow or widower, the accumulated fund is used to buy a survivor's annuity (and to provide a lump sum if more than the minimum has been going into the scheme).

APPROPRIATE PERSONAL PENSIONS

An appropriate personal pension (APP) allows you as an individual to contract out of S2P (and before April 2002 from SERPS). You and your employer pay National Insurance contributions at the full rate, but the National Insurance Contributions Office (NICO) then pays over the National Insurance rebate (see page 108), plus tax relief on the employee's share of the rebate, directly to your personal pension provider. These rebates are 'age-related', rising to 10.5 per cent of your relevant earnings (more than your National Insurance contributions) for someone currently aged 48 or over.

The fund that builds up from this part of your contributions is described as your Protected Rights, as in a COMP scheme. The money in the Protected Rights part of an APP normally has to be paid at present as an annuity and not as a lump sum (but this changes in April 2006. It has to be paid at the same rate to men and women of the same age. (Insurance companies are not required, apart from this, to offer equal annuity rates for women and men, and choose not to do so because of women's longer average life expectancy.) If the annuity was secured before April 2005, it also had to include a spouse's pension and provision for a 3 per cent increase each year for pension from contributions made before April 1997, or by 5 per cent for each year – or in line with the Retail Prices Index, if less – for pension from contributions made after that date. Since April 2005, however, you can buy a flat-rate annuity.

APPs can be taken out by any employee who is not contracted out of S2P through an employer's pension scheme. So this includes both those people who do not belong to a scheme at all, and those who belong to a scheme which is contracted in (see page 107). In this second case, however, only the money from the NI rebate can go into the APP.

Self-employed people do not belong to S2P to start with, as explained on page 56, and cannot therefore contract out with an APP.

SO WHAT SORT OF PENSION IS YOURS?

It is important, when planning to make the best of the pension arrangements you have, to know which types and categories they fall into.

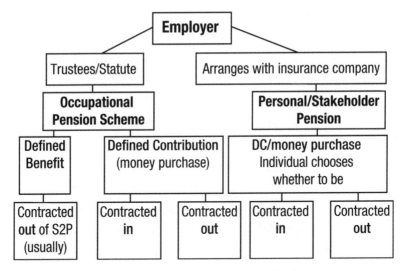

- cannot continue during career break
- can increase pension by paying AVCs (or extra contributions in some DC schemes)
- will generally have an employer contribution
- if DB, can be final salary, career average, cash balance

- can continue during career break
- can increase pension by paying extra contributions
- may have no employer contribution, or only a small one

The diagram on page 114 shows how the different types link to each other, and the table below shows who is taking what risks with the pension. One important reason for many employers changing between different types of pension is that they want to shift the risks, entirely or in part, from themselves to the employees.

Who takes the risks?		
Type of risk	Employer bears it	Individual bears it
Risk that investments do badly	Final earnings Career average Cash balance (will need to increase contributions and/or persuade employee to increase theirs, if there is not to be a shortfall)	Money purchase (will either need to increase contributions, or end up with smaller pension)
Risk that earnings rise faster than anticipated	Final earnings (will mean increased contributions) Career average/cash balance – risk shared with employee (will mean increased contributions)	Money purchase Career average/cash balance – risk shared with employer (will mean pension replaces less of pre-retirement income than expected)
Risk of increased life expectancy	Final earnings Career average (must pay pension out for longer)	Money purchase Cash balance (annuities will cost more, so pot of capital will buy less income)

✱ Action Points

For each of the non-State pensions you have – whether you are an active member now, or have a deferred or frozen pension – tick the right boxes in the table below.

	Pension X	Pension Y	Pension Z
Type			
A. Defined benefit			
i. Final salary			
ii. Career average			
iii. Cash balance			
B. Defined contribution			
Legal Framework			
C. Occupational			
i. Statutory			
ii. Trust-based			
D. Contract-based			
i. Personal			
ii. Stakeholder			
iii. Group Personal or Group Stakeholder			
E. Contracted out of S2P			
F. Contracted in to S2P			

Remember, in doing this exercise, that some of these categories are not compatible with each other. For example, if you have ticked any of the boxes against A (defined benefit), then you should have ticked one of the boxes against C (occupational) scheme, *not* against D.

You can also only be contracted out once at any one time (because you can only replace your S2P/SERPS benefit once). So if you have ticked that you are contracted out for both an occupational pension and a personal/stakeholder pension, then either:

- you have the wrong information and need to double-check; or
- a mistake was made when you started the pension, or perhaps when you got a new job and did not inform the providers of each pension about the other one. This is quite common, but best sorted out as soon as you realise.

How to find out the information

Read through your pension booklet or policy documents. Like most people, you probably looked at them once when you first received them, and then put them away after that. If you look through them again, you should find out about all the other details of what your pension provides, covered in the next few chapters of this book. Look also at your benefit statements.

Your pension scheme or provider is likely also to have a website, where there is often a wealth of information. Many such websites, for example, have calculators which allow you to see what would happen if you took early retirement, or if you increased your contributions. There will also usually be a Frequently Asked Questions (FAQs) section.

If all else fails, the booklet or website should include an address for you to contact those running the pension scheme with your queries. See also page 264 for details of how to contact the Pensions Advisory Service, which can help with many queries.

Is contracting out right for you?

If you are in a defined-benefit scheme, the decision on whether to contract out of S2P or not is made for the whole scheme, by the employer. This is also the case in the few COMP schemes that still exist, although some have separate contracted-in and contracted-out sections. If you are in a personal or stakeholder pension scheme, the decision is yours and needs to be reviewed regularly.

As illustrated on page 100, it depends largely on your age. This is because one of the most important influences on the amount of pension you receive from a DC scheme is your age when each contribution goes in. The younger you are, the more time your money has to build up interest or dividends, and so the more there will be when you retire. Or, to put it the other way round, when you are older, you have to put in much more money to achieve the same pension.

Look back at the example on page 100. If Mary wants the same amount of pension from her contribution at 40 as Bill will have from his at 20, she must put in several times as much money. For Bill, the rebate for contracting out of S2P may well be enough to give him a pension better than the State; for Mary it is much less likely to be.

By 2003, some personal pension providers were recommending policyholders not to contract out at all, whatever their age. The providers felt that the rebate was just too low, and investment returns would be too modest, to do better than the State scheme.

This age factor does not apply with defined-benefit pensions, where the accrual rate is almost always the same at all ages.

Another important issue is how much you earn, and how much you will be contributing to your pension fund. The financial institutions offering personal pensions have to pay their overheads and make a profit. So they make deductions from the contributions to cover their expenses. Since it costs nearly as much to administer a small pension fund as a large one, these deductions have tended in the past to be flat-rate, or heavily weighted against small contributors. Lower-paid people lost proportionately more, and found it more difficult to acquire an APP that offered a better return than S2P/SERPS.

However, the level of insurance companies' charges, and their structure, changed when they had to face up to the challenge of stakeholder pensions in 2002 (see pages 216–220). Since these were lower-cost and had a very simple charging structure, providers have had to cut and simplify their charges to match. It is more likely now, therefore, that a low-paid person will be able to find a personal pension to suit them than it would have been a few years ago. However, as explained on page 217, the maximum charges allowed for stakeholder schemes have now been considerably increased. The Financial Services Authority has also withdrawn the instruction that anyone selling a personal pension must be able to show that it is better for that customer than a stakeholder pension would be. Both of these changes may lead to charges creeping up again.

Women on the whole get a poorer deal out of personal pensions than men do. Annuity rates for women are lower than for men because of a woman's longer life expectancy (although the Protected Rights element of an APP has to be paid at the same rate to men and women of the same age). The other side of this is that women will get a better deal out of S2P because they draw it for longer. To limit the risks, one answer is to have a personal pension on top of S2P, rather than an APP.

For more information, see the DWP guide PM7 *Contracted-out Pensions: Your Guide,* and *Contracting Out: It's Your Choice* from the Association of British Insurers (address on page 265).

✳ Action Points

If you are contracted out via a COMP or an APP, check whether this is right for you, given your age and earnings. Ask the scheme administrator or provider if you have any doubts.

As you get older, or if your wages drop, review your decision regularly.

If the insurance company or financial adviser has written to tell you to contract back in, it will generally be wise to do so. They may be being over-cautious, to protect their backs – but they will be protecting your back too. You won't see any increase in outgoings, as your National Insurance contributions will remain the same – the money will simply be redirected from the provider to your State Pension.

If you conclude that you should now be contracted in, write to the administrator or provider to say so, and keep a copy of the letter.

THE TAX RULES

It is generally considered to be a 'good thing' in public policy terms for people to save for a non-State pension. So to encourage this, the Government gives a lot of tax relief for pension arrangements. Depending on the type of scheme, this may mean that your actual PAYE tax bill is reduced (if you belong to an occupational scheme) or that you pay the same amount of tax as you otherwise would and the provider reclaims it from HM Revenue & Customs (previously the Inland Revenue) and adds it to your account (for a personal or stakeholder pension).

The rules about tax relief have existed for years, and have grown steadily more complex as more concessions and compromises have been made. HM Revenue & Customs (HMRC) is sweeping them away from April 2006 and replacing them with a completely new set.

There will be transitional rules, mainly for the higher-paid but also for anyone who has a right to earlier-than-normal retirement.

So this section looks first at the current rules, and then at those that replace them from April 2006.

Limits for occupational pensions until April 2006

There are top limits laid down by HMRC on the amount you can receive as an occupational pension from a tax-approved scheme (a scheme under which you receive tax relief on pension contributions). The major restriction is that you cannot receive more than two-thirds of your final 'remuneration' as a pension. There is also a ceiling of £105,600 (in 2005–2006) on the annual earnings that can be taken into account (called the pensionable 'earnings cap'). Those who have earnings above this level can still receive a pension based on them, but the scheme must be 'unapproved', which means it does not receive the same tax relief. The ceiling does not affect those who were already members of their current scheme before 1 June 1989.

Finally, there is a ceiling on contributions. Employees can contribute up to 15 per cent of their earnings to an occupational scheme. Within this total, they can put money into buying 'added years', or into paying AVCs or FSAVCs to build up extra pension (all explained on pages 160–167). There is no percentage limit on the employer's contribution (except for some top executives' schemes), but they are not allowed to put in 'excessive' amounts.

At retirement, you can turn part of the pension into a lump sum (called 'commuting' the pension and covered on pages 140–142) which is tax free but limited to a figure of either 1.5 times your earnings or 2.25 times your pension (depending on when the scheme rules were agreed). The rest has to be paid as a continuing income.

Tax rules for personal pensions until April 2006

If you are not in an occupational scheme, you will be able to pay £3,600 a year (including the basic-rate tax relief given by HM Revenue & Customs) into a personal pension whether you are earning or not, and without needing to prove how much you are earning.

If you *are* in an occupational scheme and you earn less than £30,000 a year and are not a controlling director, you are allowed to put up to £3,600 a year into a stakeholder pension on top of the occupational pension limits explained on page 121.

If your earnings fluctuate, or if you have stopped work and therefore stopped earning, you can pay a contribution based on your best earnings figure within the previous five tax years.

The maximum proportion of your 'net relevant earnings' that you are allowed to pay into a personal pension rises as you get older. Net relevant earnings are total earnings for employees. For the self-employed they are their earnings less some of the deductions allowed for tax purposes.

Age at 6 April each year	Percentage of net relevant earnings that can be paid in to a personal pension that year
under 35	17.5
36–45	20
46–50	25
51–55	30
56–60	35
61–74	40

Whatever the total fund is at retirement, you can take out 25 per cent of that pot as a tax-free lump sum. The rest has to be used to buy a pension, or for you to draw a continuing income from.

The new rules after April 2006

6 April 2006 is generally being called 'A-Day' – the day when the new rules come into force. The new system will apply to occupational, personal and stakeholder pensions. Among occupational schemes, it will apply equally to DB and DC schemes (although the rules for valuing the two sorts of pension will be different). All the current limits on annual pension contributions and benefits will be replaced by a single lifetime allowance for the amount of pension saving that gets tax relief. This is under what HM Revenue & Customs describes as 'tax simplification', although when you have read through the details below you may not feel that is the right name! This section summarises what is known at present, but there may be further changes in the first few years as the system comes into operation.

✳ Action Points

Most occupational schemes and personal pension providers will be producing some information for their members on the new rules. Keep an eye out for it, and check with them about anything that might affect you.

Scheme registration

At the start of the system, all existing pension schemes of any sort will be treated automatically as 'registered' schemes, unless they choose to opt out of the new system – doing so will mean a 40 per cent tax charge on the scheme funds.

New schemes after April 2006 will have to register with HM Revenue & Customs, with a right of appeal if HMRC refuses the application.

Lifetime and annual allowances

There will be a limit on the size of pension fund (or the capital value of the pension, in a DB scheme) that each person can save without any tax penalties. This is called the Lifetime Allowance (LTA). It will start at £1.5m per person when the new arrangements are introduced in April 2006. It will be increased annually until it reaches £1.8m by 2010, and will subsequently be reviewed every five years. It is generally expected that future increases in the LTA will be in line with inflation, although this is not enshrined in law.

There are some transitional rules for people whose pensions are already over the allowance at 6 April 2006, covered on pages 133–134. There are also some other circumstances in which an individual will be given an extra percentage allowance to cover extra rights:

- rights built up over a period when the person was not a UK resident;
- transfer values from a recognised overseas pension scheme; or
- pension credits (under a divorce settlement) received before A-Day, or arising from a pension in payment acquired on or after A-Day.

As well as this Lifetime Allowance, there will be annual allowances. The 'annual allowance' is an annual limit on untaxed 'pension input' to an individual's pension fund. The allowance at A-Day will be £215,000 in 2006, but this will be increased in stages to £255,000 by 2010, and then reviewed every five years. For a DC scheme, the input is simply the contributions (not the investment returns) paid into the scheme over the year. For a DB scheme, it is the increase in the *capital* value of the individual's pension. This is worked out by taking the increase in annual pension that would be payable, and multiplying it by a factor of 10. So if, for example, at the beginning of the year your pension was worth £100 a year to you, and by the end of the year – with an extra year's accrual and a pay increase – it was worth £250, the pension input would be (£250 – £100 = £150) x 10 = £1,500.

How much of the annual allowance you have used up will have to be reported in your self-assessment tax return every year, except in the final year when you take your benefits or if you die before then.

Employees and the self-employed will get tax relief on contributions to pension schemes of all kinds up to 100 per cent of earnings or £3,600 a year, whichever is the higher. They can pay in more than this if they wish, but the extra will not get tax relief, and nor will it count against the annual allowance. It does not seem very likely that people will be able to put anything like 100 per cent of their pay into a pension as a regular thing (what would they live on, after all?), but it may be that people will put in windfall payments, perhaps from an inheritance, as they are coming up towards retirement.

How the Lifetime Allowance works

When the benefits start being paid out (now being called 'crystallised'), there is a tax charge (called the 'lifetime allowance charge') on any funds paid which are more than the LTA (but see pages 133–134 for the transitional protection). This charge is 25 per cent of the funds above the allowance, if the excess is paid out as pension, and that pension will then be taxable under PAYE. If the extra is paid out as a lump sum, the tax charge will be 55 per cent, to ensure that there is no advantage in taking the money in this way.

Crystallisation events

For most people, 'crystallising' will probably be a single event, but it will be possible to have more than one, and the funds will then be tested against the LTA each time. There are several different sorts of 'crystallisation event' and the way the funds are valued varies between them:

- **When someone starts their scheme pension** – the amount crystallised is the capital value of that pension, valued at £20 capital for every £1 of pension. So if your pension is worth £3,000, the capital value is assessed as £60,000. Some schemes may have to agree different factors with HMRC, if their pensions increase at a rate above the Retail Prices Index (RPI), or at a fixed rate of more than 5 per cent.

- **When DC funds are crystallised to start an unsecured pension (explained below), or to buy a short-term annuity** – the amount crystallised is the value of the funds turned into pension.

- **When increases are given to pensions in payment which are higher than the RPI or 5 per cent** – this is essentially to stop pension schemes for wealthy people from manipulating the system by paying a low benefit to start with and then manipulating it later. So there is an exception if the increase is given to all scheme members and there are at least 50 of them. HM Revenue & Customs has also agreed to allow annuities that give an increase as a one-off event when the member becomes seriously ill and requires long-term care.

- **When a lifetime annuity is bought** – the amount crystallised is the purchase price of the annuity.

- **On reaching 75 with benefits in a DB scheme still not 'vested'** (in other words, not yet being paid out) – the amount crystallised is the capital value of the pension, valued by the 20:1 formula, plus any additional lump sum due.

- **On taking a 'pension commencement lump sum' (the new term for tax-free cash) or a serious-ill-health lump sum** – the amount crystallised is the lump sum payable.

- **On payment of a lump-sum death benefit on death before retirement** (see pages 130–131 for death benefits).

- **On transfer to a qualifying recognised overseas pension scheme**.

For people who are already drawing a pension at the start of the new rules, the Lifetime Allowance also includes the capital value of pensions and income withdrawal (see pages 245–246) already in payment. These are valued at £25 capital for every £1 pension, to take account of the fact that tax-free cash will have been taken already.

Contracted-out rights are also covered by the LTA, but it excludes the value of any dependants' or spouses' pensions.

The pension rules after April 2006

The pension cannot be paid before the 'normal minimum pension age' (NMPA), unless the person is taking an ill-health pension. The NMPA is 50 before 6 April 2010, but 55 after that date. It will be possible to draw part of your built-up fund as pension while still working for the same employer, perhaps because you have decided to cut down your hours or take a less stressful job. Employers will not be compelled to offer this option, however. (See page 135 for the protection for those with specially early retirement ages.)

An annuity or alternatively secured pension (see below) can have a guaranteed term of 10 years – in other words, if when the individual dies the pension has been paid for less than 10 years, it can continue for the balance of that time.

People under 75 in DC schemes will have the choice of taking a scheme pension, a lifetime annuity, an unsecured pension (currently called 'income withdrawal' and covered on pages 245–246) or a short-term annuity. The scheme itself can only pay out a pension if the person has been offered the option of a lifetime annuity from the provider of their choice. This is called the 'open market option' and is covered on pages 237–238.

Before age 75, if someone in a DC scheme is withdrawing income directly from the fund rather than buying an annuity, they must not take out more than 120 per cent of the relevant annuity that could have been bought. A 'relevant annuity' is the highest annual income that could be bought for an individual of that age and sex, and must be reviewed every five years.

When someone in a DC scheme reaches age 75, they must be given a scheme pension, a lifetime annuity, or an alternatively secured pension, with the same 'open market option' as for people under 75.

If someone is taking an alternatively secured pension (in other words, withdrawing income from the fund when over 75), the amount cannot exceed more than 70 per cent of the relevant annuity they could have bought at age 75.

A defined-benefit scheme can only pay a scheme pension.

Ill-health pensions

An ill-health pension can be paid before Normal Minimum Pension Age, provided that the scheme administrator gets evidence from a registered medical practitioner that the individual is incapable of carrying on their normal occupation.

Short-term annuities

These new products will be available before the age of 75. The term must not exceed 5 years, and must finish before the individual reaches 75.

Lump-sum payments

The payment that most people are interested in is the 'pension commencement' lump sum; in other words, the money paid tax free when you start off with a pension. Whenever a scheme pension is paid, the formula for working out the maximum is complex. It is the amount of the lump sum, plus the amount crystallised to pay the scheme pension, divided by 4. In any case, it cannot be more than 25 per cent of the individual's available Lifetime Allowance. Where an annuity or an unsecured pension is being paid, it will simply be 25 per cent of the fund. Where the entitlement beginning is to a lifetime annuity, this 'applicable amount' is one-third of the annuity purchase price, including the price of any related dependant's annuity – but excluding any part of the fund representing an unsecured pension fund.

The whole of the benefit can be paid as a tax-free lump sum, subject to medical evidence that the person's life expectancy is less than a year, and providing they are under 75.

In cases where members are entitled to a refund of contributions rather than a deferred pension (see page 168), the scheme can pay these as a lump sum, but it is taxable. The tax rate is 20 per cent for the first £10,800 and 40 per cent on the remainder.

If someone has paid more than they can claim tax relief on, for example because they made a mistake about their taxable income, the scheme can refund the contributions so long as it is done within six years (although this is not compulsory).

If someone's total non-State benefits, from all sources, are worth less than 1 per cent of the LTA (so £15,000 in 2005–2006), then they are allowed to commute them in full for cash. The rules are complex, but generally 25 per cent of the cash will then be tax free, and 75 per cent taxed as earned income. Pensions in payment can also be commuted under this rule, but they will be taxed in full as earned income.

When an occupational scheme winds up, members' benefits that are worth less than 1 per cent of the LTA (so £15,000 in 2005–2006) may be paid as lump sums so long as the member is under 75. The employer has to give an undertaking to HMRC that it will not contribute to another scheme, in respect of that member, for a year after paying the lump sum. Twenty-five per cent of the cash will then be tax free, and 75 per cent taxed as earned income. HM Revenue & Customs says that schemes must not be wound up simply in order to pay out lump sums, and can potentially fine trustees up to £3,000 for each member who gets the lump sum.

Death benefits

There are no fewer than nine different sorts of death benefit under the new rules, each with a new label as well.

The death benefits from uncrystallised funds are:

i. **Uncrystallised funds lump-sum death benefit**. This is the amount in the member's account in a DC scheme, which can be paid as a lump sum if the member dies before age 75.

ii **Defined-benefits lump-sum death benefit**. This is the lump sum promised in a DB scheme if the member dies before age 75.

Both of these have to be paid within two years of the member's death, and are then tested against the individual's LTA.

iii **Trivial commutation lump-sum death benefits**. A dependant's pension entitlements can be paid as a lump sum if their total value is within 1 per cent of the LTA and is paid before the deceased member's 75th birthday.

iv **Winding-up lump-sum death benefit**. A scheme that is winding up is allowed to pay any dependant's pension entitlement valued at less than 1 per cent of the LTA as a lump sum.

The death benefits from crystallised funds are:

i   **Unsecured pension funds lump-sum death benefit**. If someone dies while drawing an unsecured pension before age 75, the residual value can be paid as a lump sum, but there will be a 35 per cent tax charge.

ii **Annuity protection lump-sum death benefit**. If a member of a DC scheme dies before age 75, and has bought a lifetime annuity, it will be possible for the provider to pay out the unused capital, but there will be a 35 per cent tax charge.

iii **Pension protection lump-sum death benefit**. This is, broadly, a return of capital under a DB scheme if a member dies before age 75 whilst drawing a pension.

iv **Charity lump-sum death benefit**. If someone who is drawing an alternatively secured income dies at or after 75 without dependants, their funds may be left to a charity nominated by them. The Treasury has said, however, that it is considering imposing Inheritance Tax charges in these cases, although it is still considering the details of how it would do this.

v   **Transfer lump-sum death benefit**. If someone who is drawing an alternatively secured income dies on or after 75 without dependants, their funds may be left to another scheme member, with the scheme administrator selecting the person if they have not nominated anyone. The Government is looking at the Inheritance Tax rules that will apply to transfer lump-sum death benefits and the Treasury is considering Inheritance Tax charges (see above).

Liability for any tax charge after a member's death will fall on the recipients of the money, with HM Revenue & Customs deciding what proportion each individual should bear.

Going abroad

There are also new rules on 'migrant member relief', which means tax relief for people going to work abroad, or for people from other countries coming to work here. These are complex, but, broadly, they will give people in these situations much more opportunity than at present to pay into UK pension schemes and receive tax relief.

✴ Action Points

Check with your employer or with an accountant if you think the migrant members' rules might be relevant to you.

Penalties and unauthorised payments

There are various penalties for different types of non-compliance with the legislation, including penalties for false statements, documents and information. There is also the risk of having to meet tax charges for unauthorised payments. Examples of these might be:

- attempts to assign policies to someone else;
- holding assets to benefit members and their families other than by payment of scheme benefits;
- 'value shifting'– in other words, transactions which pass value from the scheme to the member; or
- unauthorised payments to the employer, or borrowing by the employer from the scheme.

Investments

A loan can be made to the sponsoring employer, provided that:

- it is not worth more than 50 per cent of the market value of the scheme's assets;
- it is secured by a charge of adequate value;
- a commercial rate of interest is being paid; and
- the loan is for a term of not more than five years, although there is one opportunity to extend the term by up to a further five years.

Schemes can also borrow up to 50 per cent of the value of scheme assets. Any borrowing above this level will lead to a 40 per cent tax charge.

A wide range of investments will be allowed, including in residential property. This is being seen as a new opportunity for people running small businesses or with capital to spare to maximise their tax relief via their pension fund. There seems in particular to be a bandwagon rolling for arrangements to invest in housing. Anyone attracted by this must take professional advice, as there are numerous pitfalls.

Your tax return after April 2006

Individuals are responsible for checking whether they come within the contribution limits, and they will be required to make a declaration when they join a registered scheme. They must declare details of any contributions that do not qualify for tax relief, on their annual self-assessment returns, and new guidance will be issued for this.

Transitional protection for those with large funds

People whose pension benefits are worth more than the £1.5m LTA may apply to protect existing benefits, provided they are within current HM Revenue & Customs limits as at 5 April 2006.

This can be done through either 'Primary' or 'Enhanced' Protection:

- **Primary Protection** can be utilised by anyone whose total pension valued at A-Day is greater than £1.5 million. Your Lifetime Allowance will be higher than £1.5 million and will enable you to continue to build up further pension. A recovery charge may be payable on part of the pension above your LTA.

- **Enhanced Protection** is an alternative to Primary Protection and is also available for people whose benefits are not over £1.5 million on 5 April 2006, but who think that they may become so in future. If you go for this, then after 6 April 2006 you must not build up any more pension benefits in your current arrangement, or any other arrangement. However, this protection is intended to guarantee that your benefits are exempt from any recovery charge.

If you apply for either Primary or Enhanced Protection, your tax-free cash entitlement prior to A-Day may also be protected.

The decision to apply for either protection will be yours. In order to make this decision, you will require certain information about your benefits from your current and previous pension schemes. Once you have collected all the information that you need from each scheme, you will be able to see if the value of your benefits exceeds the Lifetime Allowance. You will have three years from 6 April 2006 to register your funds for protection. If you wish to consider Enhanced Protection, you must still make up your mind *before* 6 April 2006 in order to stop building up any further pension from A-Day.

Pension schemes and providers should be giving all their members statements of their benefits, so that they can decide whether they need to apply or not, and if so for which type of protection.

✱ Action Points

If you think there is any chance that you will be affected by the Lifetime Allowance, ask your scheme administrator for a statement, and get financial advice. The earlier you do this the better, because advisers will get very busy in the run-up to the changeover.

Protected pension ages

People who had a *right* to take their benefits (without needing the trustees' or employer's consent) before the age of 55 from their schemes under the old system have that right protected. For those in occupational schemes, the conditions are that:

- they must have been in the scheme, and had the right to take their pension before 55, on or before 5 April 2006; and
- the rules of the scheme gave them this right on or before 10 December 2003 (or would have given it, if they had been members of the scheme by then).

Protected members must take all their benefits at once, when no longer working for the employer. They will lose the protection if they transfer out of the scheme as individuals, although 'bulk transfers' (when a whole group of people are transferred at once, perhaps because of the sale of a business) do not affect it.

People with personal pensions have similar rights, if their job was one of those listed by HMRC as having a special early retirement age. This covers occupations such as ballet-dancing and professional football. Again, they must take all their benefits at once.

In most cases, where the protected pension age is below 50, the Lifetime Allowance is reduced by 2.5 per cent for each year before the Normal Minimum Pension Age by which the member leaves early. However, the regulations exempt members of the armed forces, police and fire service from this reduction.

✱ Action Points

Check whether you are covered by these rules – look in your scheme documents, or ask your scheme administrator.

If you are, think about whether you need to take the reduction in the Lifetime Allowance (unless you are in an exempt group) into account in your forward planning.

Get advice if necessary, from your union or your scheme administrator.

OCCUPATIONAL PENSIONS

Around 10 million employees – just under half the working population – are currently active members of occupational pension schemes (also called 'company' pension schemes or, formerly in the public sector, 'superannuation'). Around six million people receive payments from such schemes. Over half the people who have retired in recent years have had some sort of occupational pension, although the coverage of occupational schemes is now declining.

This chapter looks at how occupational schemes work, and the benefits that come from them. It also covers issues for women, and for anyone who wants either to retire early or to work on after retirement age. Finally, it covers the important question of security – the recent legal changes which mean that even if your employer disappears, you will receive benefits from the contributions you have paid in.

HOW OCCUPATIONAL SCHEMES WORK

Many employers, especially the larger ones, offer an occupational pension to their employees as part of their package of non-wage benefits. There are two main ways of doing this:

- through an occupational pension scheme (also called a 'company scheme' or 'superannuation'), covered in this chapter; or
- through a Group Personal Pension (GPP) or stakeholder pension.

As explained in the previous chapter, occupational pensions can be either 'defined benefit' or 'defined contribution' (DB or DC). As the majority of people who are in occupational schemes are covered by the defined-benefit arrangements (in most cases, final-salary), these are covered first in each section, with any differences for defined-contribution (DC) schemes incorporated in shaded boxes.

Until the tax changes on 6 April 2006, both DC and DB schemes are covered by the same HMRC top limits on the amounts of benefit they can give in different circumstances. For DB schemes in particular, this means that the benefits were often closely modelled on the HM Revenue & Customs rules, even if they gave less than the maximum that HMRC would have allowed. Although they will have much more flexibility in the future, the majority of schemes will probably not change very much.

Two major changes are likely to be that:

- schemes will increase to the maximum the tax-free lump sum that they allow members to take; and
- death-in-service benefits may well be paid more in lump-sum form and less as pension, because for most people the tax treatment will be more favourable. (The pension would be taxed under PAYE while the lump sum is payable free of Income Tax.)

Defined-benefit pensions

An example of how a *final-salary* pension formula works was given on page 94. To see how it works out in your own scheme, you need to know three things:

- the accrual rate;
- the definitions of 'pensionable' and 'final pensionable' salary; and
- what your 'pensionable service' is.

You should be able to find the various definitions from the pension scheme booklet. Ask your scheme administrator if they are not clear.

The 'accrual rate' is the fraction of your final pensionable earnings you receive for every year of scheme membership, usually $\frac{1}{60}$ or $\frac{1}{80}$ (sometimes expressed as a percentage). With an accrual rate of $\frac{1}{80}$ you will normally have to belong to a scheme for 40 years to get a pension of half these earnings ($\frac{40}{80}$). If the accrual rate is $\frac{1}{60}$, 40 years in the scheme will entitle you to $\frac{40}{60}$ – in other words, two-thirds of your earnings at retirement. Some schemes have different accrual rates for different ages, or allow you to choose different rates (and contribution levels).

Your 'final pensionable earnings' may be an average of your earnings over the last two or three years, or years further back if your earnings have dropped as you come up to retirement. Some schemes provide a pension based on earnings in the last 12 months, or in the last tax year. Sometimes only part of your pay is pensionable. Schemes may be 'integrated' or have 'clawback' with the State Basic Pension – meaning that they deduct an amount from your pay linked to the State Pension, before calculating the pension. Alternatively, the scheme's pension may be calculated on the basis of your full pay, but then have all, or a proportion of, the State Basic Pension deducted from it. Not surprisingly, this is very unpopular with members and there are a number of campaigns against it. Features like this can make a sizeable difference to the amount you get, so check the scheme booklet.

A person's length of membership in a pension scheme is still usually called by the old-fashioned name of 'service' in many scheme booklets and benefit statements. In some schemes you join as soon as you become an employee. Others say that you must wait, perhaps as long as five years, or must be over a certain age.

For *career-average* and *cash-balance* schemes (explained on pages 95–98) there will be similar definitions, although these may be called by different names. You also need to understand the pension formula. These formulae can be very complex, and vary considerably between schemes. With the newer schemes, in most cases a lot of effort has gone into scheme communication and the employer is probably spending a lot of money on the scheme, but is not getting value for money if people do not appreciate it because they do not understand it.

✷ Action Points

If you have made an effort to understand your pension and not succeeded, the chances are that a lot of other people are in the same boat. So ask the scheme administrator, or the trustees, to organise some presentations for the members, and/or some 'surgeries' where members can have a discussion one-to-one about their concerns.

Lump sums on retirement

Almost every pension scheme in the private sector, and some in the public sector, allow you to turn part of your pension into a lump sum on retirement, and this is tax free. This is called 'commuting' the pension. Your scheme booklet should tell you what the commutation factors are. These are the amount of cash you would get for each £1 of pension given up – in effect, the price at which you sell the pension back to the scheme. This can vary considerably with age and sex, and depends on how generous the scheme is, but a typical figure might be somewhere between £9 and £12 of cash for each £1 given up by a man aged 65, or more for women and for people retiring early.

Until April 2006, the HMRC rules are that you can normally take ‰ of your final earnings for each year of service up to a maximum of 40 years. Alternatively, your scheme can allow you to take a lump sum that is two and a quarter times your annual pension worked out before commutation. Some schemes allow anyone with service of 20 years or more to take the maximum amount – check your own scheme rules. However, your Guaranteed Minimum Pension – or Protected Rights Pension in a contracted-out money-purchase (COMP) scheme – currently has to be taken as a pension, and cannot be commuted to a lump sum, although these rules will change in April 2006. (At time of writing, the full details are not yet known.) There are also limits on commuting pension you build up from Additional Voluntary Contributions (AVCs), as explained on page 163, but these also change in April 2006.

In some public service schemes, such as those in local government and the NHS, it is almost automatic that you receive both a pension (smaller than a good private sector pension) and a lump sum. There are some exceptions in cases where you join the scheme as a late entrant. There is therefore generally no need to 'commute' any of your pension. In theory, the scheme rules often allow you to turn part of your lump sum back into pension, but the lure of the tax-free money is such that it is hardly ever done. With the reforms currently under way in public sector schemes, this is likely to change and schemes will come into line with the private sector.

Under the HM Revenue & Customs pension tax reforms (as explained on pages 123–136) in 2006, the maximum lump sum is likely to be more than most people would be allowed under the current rules, and in many cases much larger.

Should you take the lump sum?

Almost everyone does take the lump sum at retirement, because it is tax free and very tempting. It is worth thinking about more, however. The level of commutation factors has not kept up with increased life expectancy, and so schemes make a profit on it. A neutral commutation factor in a good scheme might be £15 per £1 given up, or even higher. So in effect it is the scheme, not the member, who benefits from the lump sum being tax free.

✳ Action Points

At retirement, think about what lump sum you *need*, rather than what you would like to have. Consider whether it would be better to take less than the maximum you could have, and so have a better pension to live on.

As part of this, think about how long you are likely to live, and what increases the scheme will pay to take account of inflation.

Contributions

Usually, both employer and employees contribute to the pension scheme, but some schemes are 'non-contributory'. This means that the employer alone contributes. They are more common in the financial services industry than elsewhere, and among senior executives.

In recent years, many schemes have increased employees' contributions, or brought in new contribution rules where there were none before, because of the increased cost of schemes. (See pages 192–195 for details of what rights you have if the employer wants to change your scheme.)

Defined-contribution pensions

In a defined-contribution scheme, as explained on pages 98–100, there is no promise of a particular level of pension; instead, what you get depends on what money has gone into the scheme, and how well it is invested. So the important points to look for in your scheme booklet are:

Contributions

- How much can you contribute, and how much does the employer contribute?

- If the scheme is contracted out of S2P (explained on pages 111–113), do those figures include the National Insurance rebate, or are they additional to them?

In many cases, the contributions are 'tiered' or 'matched' so that those who opt to pay more get a bigger contribution from the employer as well. For example, there might be flexibility about the amount the employee puts in, with a minimum contribution of 3 per cent. The employer may be offering to match what the employee puts in, perhaps up to 6 per cent. In that case, it makes sense to put in at least 6 per cent, to lever in the maximum amount from the employer, if you can afford it.

Investments

- What choice of investments do you have? (The range available is usually the same as for personal pensions, explained on pages 207–210.)

- Can you switch between them?

- Does the company make financial advice available? (It can get some tax relief for arranging for workplace financial advice.)

- What are the charges, and who pays them?

Benefit structure

- At what age is the full pension payable?

- What happens if you retire early?

- What benefit is there if you have to retire due to ill-health (see pages 185–186)?

Taking a lump sum

In a defined-contribution scheme, you can take part of the fund as a lump sum on retirement. The same tax rules as for defined-benefit pensions apply, up to 6 April 2006. After that, the general rules explained on pages 123–136 will apply, and you will be able to take 25 per cent of the fund as a lump sum.

However, if you are in a COMP scheme (explained on pages 111–113), you cannot take any of your Protected Rights fund as cash. This changes from April 2006, when you will be allowed to do so if it is 'trivial', or if you are suffering from very serious ill-health (where your expectation of life is a year or less). In both cases, you will then pay tax on the extra part of the pension.

Benefit at retirement

At retirement, whatever money is in your 'pot' will be used to buy an annuity. This might be bought from an insurance company, or, if it is a large scheme, it may provide this itself. In general after April 2006 you will have an 'open market option' (OMO, explained on pages 237–238), which means that you should be able to shop around for the best annuity rate available.

✳ Action Points

Check your DC scheme booklet and website carefully, and establish where your money is being invested.

Think about whether this is suitable for you; for example, are you happy with the risk levels?

Check whether financial advice or information is available through the scheme (and press for it to be made available if it is not).

At regular intervals, decide whether you can afford to put more into your DC scheme through increasing your contributions.

Decide too whether the investment mix is right for you, or whether you should switch between the different categories of investment.

At retirement, check whether there is an open market option, and ensure that you (or the trustees on your behalf) shop around to find the best annuity available for you.

Small self-administered schemes

For small businesses, the small self-administered scheme (SSAS) is an option worth considering, as it allows you to make larger pension contributions while still using the money in your business.

'Self-investment' – investing in the employing company's shares, loans to the company, or property occupied by it – of more than 5 per cent of the fund is not generally allowed in occupational pension schemes. In an SSAS, however, a far higher proportion of the fund can be used to buy assets for the business, such as an office or building from which it is run. The business then pays rent to the fund.

An SSAS can have no more than 11 members in all, and if the 'self-investment' option is used, then all members must be trustees, and all trustees' decisions must be unanimous. There must also be an outside 'pensioneer' trustee (an expert who is there to see that HMRC's special rules for these schemes are obeyed).

Anyone contemplating this sort of arrangement should obtain specialist advice from an actuarial firm. Setting-up costs are high, and unlikely to be worthwhile unless the total annual contribution is at least £20,000.

The HM Revenue & Customs rule changes in April 2006 (see pages 123–136) will affect SSASs in the same way as for other types of pension. If you are thinking of setting up an SSAS now, it will be important to check with your adviser how the tax reforms could affect your plans.

✱ Action Points

If you run a small business, think about whether an SSAS is a suitable way to make pension provision for yourself and colleagues. If you already have an SSAS or are thinking of getting one, get advice on how the tax changes will affect you.

SHOULD YOU JOIN YOUR EMPLOYER'S PENSION SCHEME?

The answer is generally yes. Although such schemes vary considerably in quality, the employer will always pay in contributions (over the long term, even if not currently). Not joining, therefore, in effect means giving money back to the employer. Defined-benefit schemes also protect your pension against inflation, completely or in part, at least during your working life.

There is, however, the question of security to be considered. A statutory scheme, such as the Teachers' Scheme or the NHS Scheme, is totally safe because it is guaranteed by the Government. In the private sector, however, you may want to look at whether the scheme has a deficit and what the employer is doing about it, and to ask specifically if there are any plans to close the scheme down (see page 190 for an explanation of what happens then). You are also likely to be given additional benefits such as a spouse's pension, a lump-sum death benefit, and a pension if you have to retire because of ill-health. Therefore, provided that the contribution rate is not too high, you are likely to get value for money even if the worst happens and the scheme is wound up, when you take into account the value of these 'insurance' elements.

Should you join a DC scheme?

For DC schemes, again the answer is generally yes. The employer will usually be paying in contributions, and there are normally extra benefits for death and ill-health. The exception might be if the scheme is a low-quality COMP (see pages 111–113), with little or nothing extra going in beyond the National Insurance rebate. Then, even for a younger person the benefits of joining would be marginal, or even negative, given current investment forecasts, and older people would want to be very cautious about doing so.

The official regulatory bodies take the view that there would need to be a very good reason for someone with an employer's scheme (of any sort) available to them to reject the chance of joining and to buy a personal or stakeholder pension instead. The only group for whom this might not be true are people who are sure they will stay less than two years with the employer (for example those on short-term contracts).

However, no one has to join an employer's scheme. You could rely on S2P or take out a personal or stakeholder pension. As already pointed out, S2P on its own will not produce a good retirement income. So the real choice is between an employer's scheme, if available, and a personal pension. Personal pensions are described in detail in the next chapter; stakeholder pensions are explained on pages 216–220.

For more information, see the FSA *Guide to the Risks of Opting Out of your Employer's Pension Scheme.*

What if you're low-paid?

If your earnings are low, you may feel that you cannot afford to join the pension scheme on offer from your employer. Many women in particular feel that they will be able to rely on their husbands' pensions. But you can never be sure that your marriage will last, and joining the scheme will often add some financial protection in the event of death or ill-health. With the tax relief on contributions, the actual cost of joining the pension scheme in your own right is not high.

✱ Action Points

If you work for an employer where there is a pension scheme, and you are not a member:

- Find out whether you are eligible, or will become so in the future. You may want to press for a change, if the rules are restrictive.
- Think carefully before deciding *not* to join, and discuss it with your spouse or partner.
- If the problem is affordability, work out what the *real* cost of joining is, after you have taken account of the savings you make on tax and National Insurance. You may be able to find a calculator on the scheme's website to do this for you, or the scheme administrator may be able to help.

ISSUES FOR WOMEN

Equal treatment for men and women

In the past, there used to be considerable discrimination against women in employer-run pension schemes. This has slowly been changing, but there are still many areas where women get a poorer deal than men do. The fact that women's earnings tend to be lower than men's means that they also end up with lower pensions.

Women in DC schemes

The law on equal treatment of men and women is broadly the same as for DB schemes. One exception is that, in DC schemes, women's longer life expectancy means that the 'pot' of money available for pensions has to last longer, so women receive smaller annuities than men for the same lump sum. European law is still not completely clear about this, but it does look as if such discrimination is permitted. For a COMP scheme (explained on pages 111–113), they do have to be calculated on a 'unisex' basis, however.

In 1990 the European Court of Justice took a landmark decision that pensions must be regarded as pay for the purposes of the laws on equal treatment. It was in fact a man who brought the case, about one of the areas where men lose out – early retirement (see below). A series of other test cases clarified some of the disputed issues about equality in September 1994. To summarise a rather complex position, it appears that:

- If a scheme has been providing unequal benefits for men and women or unequal pension ages, the 'disadvantaged sex' can claim improvements up to the level of the better-off sex, for service since 17 May 1990.

- However, when the employer changes the rules for future service to bring them into line with equal-treatment requirements, they are allowed to reduce benefits for the advantaged sex, to bring them down to the level of the disadvantaged sex.
- There are exceptions for actuarially calculated figures, such as early-retirement reduction, commutation payments and transfer payments. There are also exceptions where an unequal benefit is there to compensate for unequal State benefits. In particular, a scheme which provides a 'bridging pension' equivalent to the State Pension is allowed to pay this to men between the ages of 60 and 65 but not to women.
- Part-timers have in the past often been excluded from employers' pension schemes. The European Court of Justice has ruled that this can be indirect discrimination if it affects more women than men and there is no 'objective justification' for it.

So the position now in the UK is that:

- You have up to six months after leaving a job to make a claim that there was indirect discrimination (or you can put in a claim at any time while in that job).
- If you have had a series of linked short-term contracts, the six months only starts to run when the employment relationship ends altogether. However, the definition of this is very tight, and you will fall outside it if you had a break in your employment for your own reasons rather than those of the employer.

You can claim for arrears right back to 1976, but if you would have been paying contributions during that time, the scheme is entitled to claim these off you in return. However, under UK regulations the employer must pay the whole cost for any service after 31 May 1995.

> ## ✱ Action Points
>
> If you are still at work, or have only recently left, there is still an opportunity to put in an Equal Treatment claim if you were discriminated against as a part-timer in the past. Contact your union, or the Pensions Advisory Service (TPAS) at the address on page 264, before doing so. It may be possible to negotiate a deal on this without needing to go through the legal formalities.
>
> If your employer has altered your pension rights in a way that it is not legally entitled to do, you can put in a claim to have your rights reinstated. You may be able to challenge unfair treatment in future, at any time before the date when you would originally have retired, if you do not want to cause friction with your employer now. Ask the scheme administrator for details of the current position.
>
> Very large numbers of Employment Tribunal claims were put in during the 1990s by women who had lost out on pensions because part-timers were excluded from membership of the scheme. Most have now been settled, but if you have a claim that is still ongoing, consult your union if you receive any correspondence from the Employment Tribunal about it.

Part-time work

Under the *Employment Relations Act 1999*, part-time employees must not be treated less favourably than full-time staff doing comparable jobs, on pensions as on other issues. This should make it easier to challenge schemes that still prevent part-timers from joining, and should lead to the redesign of many schemes.

However, if you work part-time your earnings will be low, which means that your pension from your employer will also be low. In addition, some pension schemes penalise part-timers in the way that the pension is calculated. These are so-called 'integrated' schemes, where the equivalent of the State Basic Pension is deducted from the pensionable salary to start with. This has a relatively greater effect on part-timers with low earnings than on full-time employees who earn more. It is legal for the scheme to be designed in this way, even if it does hit women harder than men. Try to put pressure on the employer to change this if it applies to you.

Family leave and pensions

Pregnant women in the UK, regardless of the hours they work or their length of service, must be given 26 weeks' paid maternity leave. For the first six weeks of that they are entitled to 90 per cent of their ordinary pay, after which the statutory level goes down to £100 (although many collective agreements do better). During this time their contractual rights, including pension rights, must be maintained. Occupational pension schemes must also make other periods of paid maternity leave pensionable, as if you are receiving your usual rate of pay.

Contributions can only be deducted, however, on the basis of the pay you are actually receiving. (For example, if your normal earnings are £200 a week, and your maternity pay is only £100 a week, your pension must build up as if you are earning £200, but your contributions can only be deducted on the basis of the £100 you are actually getting.)

Employers do not have to provide any pension benefits during periods of unpaid leave, but the scheme rules will often say that periods of unpaid leave will be credited if the employee pays her share of the contributions, or they can make no provision for this (so long as anyone else on unpaid leave is treated in the same way). Even if the period of leave is not pensionable, you should be treated as having continuous service for the periods on each side of the gap, and not as having left and returned.

There is also now (since 6 April 2003) a right to adoption leave, for men and women. They must have worked for the employer for at least 26 weeks to be eligible, and are then entitled to up to 26 weeks' ordinary (paid) adoption leave and 26 weeks' additional (unpaid) leave.

There is also a right for men to take paid paternity leave, although this is only two weeks.

Finally, there is also 'parental' leave, for those who have been employed by that employer for a year and have responsibility for a child under 5 (or 18 for a disabled child). This is up to 13 weeks in total (18 weeks for a disabled child), but the employer can say that no more than 4 weeks should be taken in any one year.

There used to be differences in the pensions treatment of all these different sorts of family leave, but in April 2005, the rules were harmonised with those for maternity leave, explained above.

Maternity and family leave and DC schemes

For periods of paid maternity leave and the other sorts of family leave, there is some legal doubt about how much the contributions by the employer should be. If these are reduced because your pay is less, then your pension will also be less. The Government's view is that employers do not have to make up the gap, but some lawyers have different views. The question will not be settled until there is a test case on the matter.

DEATH BENEFITS

Lump-sum benefit

Generally, there is a lump-sum 'death benefit' or 'life-assurance benefit' if a member of an occupational scheme of any type dies at any time while working for that employer. Sometimes this benefit, perhaps at a lower level, also covers people who are too young, or have not worked for the employer for long enough, to join the scheme yet.

Up to April 2006, HM Revenue & Customs allows schemes to pay a maximum death benefit of four times the member's earnings, plus a refund of the member's contributions with interest. Occupational schemes will be allowed to pay much bigger lump sums on death after that date, as explained on pages 130–131. Whether they will actually do so is another matter.

This lump sum is usually paid to a 'beneficiary' nominated by the member or selected by the trustees. There is usually a nomination form in the scheme booklet or available from the pensions administrator. It could also be called an 'expression of wish form' or a 'letter of wishes'. These names make clear one important point – it is the trustees, not the member, who have the final decision on where the money should go. This is for two reasons: firstly, it means that the money is not technically the property of the member at the point of death, so it is not caught for Inheritance Tax. Secondly, it allows the trustees to take the real circumstances into account, if perhaps someone has not changed their nomination for many years or has asked for something that seems unreasonable. The trustees have a duty to act as 'reasonable and prudent people, not frivolously or maliciously', but, nonetheless, many people do resent their involvement in this.

✳ Action Points

If you want to be as sure as you can that they will follow your wishes:

- keep your nomination form up to date, and review it whenever your circumstances change; and
- if you are asking the trustees to do something which they might think unusual, add a letter explaining the reasons.

Example

Laurence is a widower, with two sons who are doing very well for themselves and one who has never been able to hold down a job, as he has bouts of very bad depression. Laurence has agreed with the two other sons that they will always look after the third, and so he wants the pension scheme's death benefit to go to them jointly, to be held in trust for the third. He puts the bare facts on his nomination form, and adds a letter signed by all his sons, spelling out what they have agreed.

In some public sector pension schemes, however, the lump sum is treated as part of your estate, so you can leave it in your will.

Once an employee reaches retirement age, this life-assurance benefit usually disappears, although there are a few schemes which offer a flat-rate 'funeral benefit'. The HMRC rules say that the maximum payable is £2,500. Under the new tax rules explained on pages 123–136, after April 2006 provision of a funeral benefit will only be allowed where the member is aged under 75. However, the transitional rules will let it continue for people who had already retired before 6 April 2006, and where the provision was in the scheme rules before 10 December 2003.

Five-year guarantee

Most schemes have a five-year guarantee. This means that if a member dies in the first five years of retirement, the unpaid balance of five years' pension can be given as a lump sum, or possibly a continuing pension. This lump-sum balance is often paid in addition to any survivor's pension that is to come into immediate payment. A lump sum may be the full balance of the five years' money or it may be 'discounted'. This means that the amount may be reduced to take account of the interest the fund could have earned on the money over the years if it had not been paid out all at once.

Under the new HMRC rules, this lump sum (called a pension protection lump sum) will be taxable (at 35 per cent) if paid after 6 April 2006. Some schemes may therefore change to provide an option for the member's pension to continue for the balance of the five years.

Pensions for dependants

If a scheme member dies in service, there is usually a pension for a widow or widower. The HMRC's (pre-April 2006) rules allow this to be a maximum of two-thirds of the member's projected pension based on service to the normal retirement date. When pensions for children are added, the total must not exceed the member's maximum projected pension. However, most earnings-related schemes give a half pension rather than two-thirds, and many money-purchase schemes give only a pension bought out of the fund that has built up for the member by the time they die. This could be very small if the member is young.

When the death takes place after retirement, there is usually also a widow's or widower's pension. This may be half or two-thirds of the member's own pension. However, it is usually based on the full pension entitlement before any reduction because a lump sum has been taken – and as uprated, once in payment.

Civil Partnerships

As explained on pages 39–40, the new *Civil Partnerships Act* comes into force in December 2005. Schemes which are contracted out of S2P will have to give the minimum required spouse's benefits from that date, taking account of the member's service back to 1988. However, members may want to put pressure on their schemes to go further than this. When widowers' pensions came in from 1988 onwards, the more generous schemes gave them on the basis of the member's full service and under the same conditions as for widows – you may want to try to persuade them to do the same for civil partners.

It will also be worth asking whether the scheme provides for unmarried partners, and if not why not. If it starts to do so, then to avoid falling foul of anti-discrimination laws, the benefits must be payable to both same-sex and opposite-sex partners.

Death benefits and DC schemes

For the lump-sum death benefit, the position is the same as for the defined-benefit schemes explained above.

For the spouse's pension, a COMP scheme (explained on pages 111–113) has to provide a Protected Rights pension. Other defined-contribution schemes do not have to offer any spouse's pension. The more generous ones will provide one based on a proportion of the member's salary, perhaps 25 per cent or 30 per cent.

Alternatively, the fund built up may be used to buy an annuity for the spouse. (Annuities are explained on pages 237–244.) The younger the spouse is, the lower the payment will be in return for the same size of fund, because the money has to be stretched further.

DC schemes can also provide benefits for unmarried partners, and the position on Civil Partnerships is the same as for DB schemes, explained above.

✳ Action Points

Check that the death benefits offered by your own scheme are adequate. If not, raise the matter with the scheme trustees.

If you and your partner are not married, check whether the spouse's pension can be paid to a 'financial dependant'. Many schemes do not allow for this. This will make it even more important to complete, and keep up to date, a nomination form for the death benefit, so that at least the lump sum can be paid to your partner.

Check what the scheme is doing about Civil Partnerships and press the trustees to take a generous view.

OCCUPATIONAL PENSIONS AND DIVORCE

In the past, it was not possible to divide an occupational pension between a husband and wife who got divorced. The law has changed twice in recent years, however.

Earmarking

Where the divorce process was started after July 1996, it is possible to 'earmark' part of an occupational pension for a former spouse. This means that once the pension starts being paid, it is divided between the member and the former spouse according to a judge's order. It dies with the member, however, and if the former spouse remarries he or she loses it.

Earmarking is complicated and does not work very well, so there have been very few orders made.

Pension sharing

For divorces where the petition was issued after 1 December 2000, 'pension sharing' is now available. This means that an occupational, stakeholder or personal pension can be divided at the time of divorce, and the former spouse will generally then be able to transfer it elsewhere.

Pension sharing means that:

- As part of the information-gathering for the financial settlement, the scheme member will be asked to obtain details of the transfer value (explained on page 172) from the pension scheme.
- The court may make an order that part of this transfer value is passed over to the other spouse.
- Depending on the type of scheme it is, and the policy the trustees have adopted, the other spouse may then have to leave it with the member's scheme for them to look after, transfer it to his or her own scheme or a personal pension, or have a choice of doing either. (Information about which options are available in any particular scheme will be included along with the details of the transfer value.)
- Until April 2006, the amount that has been passed over to the other spouse is treated as if it is still part of the original member's pension, so is not counted against the HM Revenue & Customs maximum for the former spouse. However, this rule is being reversed in 2006, as part of HMRC's pensions tax reforms, as explained on pages 123–136. From then on, the amount passed across will be treated as an addition to the other spouse's pension to be counted against the Lifetime Allowance, and a reduction in the original member's pension.

Where both spouses are young, or both have roughly equal pensions, the courts are unlikely to make a pension order. It is where one person has a much greater pensions entitlement than the other – a senior civil servant whose wife has been working part-time while looking after young children, for example – that it will apply. Even then, if there are other assets, such as the value of an owner-occupied house or a share portfolio, it is more likely that these will be divided, as it is simpler and clearer.

✳ Action Points

It is *essential* that anyone thinking of getting a divorce in a situation where one or other party has substantial pension rights, gets legal assistance. The rules, and the forms that need filling in to give information to the courts, are complex and it is easy to make mistakes.

BUYING EXTRA PENSION

Employees aiming for a pension worth two-thirds of their final pensionable earnings need to spend 40 years in a pension scheme that gives $\frac{1}{60}$ of salary for each year of service. If you have had a varied or broken career pattern, your pension benefits could be far smaller. If your pension is based on $\frac{1}{80}$ of final earnings, then 40 years will give you only half pay. The calculation of the pension may in any case be based on less than total earnings. You may therefore want to think about making extra contributions to your pension scheme, or about paying into another (stakeholder) scheme in addition.

The older you are, the less time you have to contribute to a pension fund and for your contribution to grow in value. So if you are paying the extra over only a short period, you will need to put in a considerable amount. This may not be as unrealistic as it sounds, since an older person may well have fewer financial commitments. At the same time, the need for an adequate retirement income becomes more apparent. Once the pension tax reforms explained on pages 123–136 come in, from April 2006, most people will have the room to put money into their pension schemes in the last few years before they retire.

The current position

Until April 2006 there are a limited number of ways in which you can build up extra pension if you are in an occupational pension scheme. These are:

- buying added years (if you are in a public sector scheme, or one of a few private sector ones which allow for this);
- paying Additional Voluntary Contributions (AVCs);
- paying Free-Standing Additional Voluntary Contributions (FSAVCs);
- if you have earned less than £30,000 in any of the five previous tax years, excluding any tax year before 2000–2001, and are not a controlling director, paying up to £3,600 a year into a personal or stakeholder pension scheme; or
- taking a 'salary sacrifice' in return for higher pension contributions from the employer.

The picture changes considerably after April 2006, however.

Added years

In public sector schemes such as those for teachers or the NHS, you can pay extra contributions over a period, or all at once as a lump sum, to buy extra pension and lump sum. This is quite expensive, because it is valuable. You buy extra years or parts of years of service, which means an increased pension linked to your final salary, for yourself and your spouse, with full inflation-proofing. You take no investment risk.

A few private sector schemes, particularly those in the former nationalised industries, also have provisions for this.

> ### ✳ Action Points
>
> Look in your scheme booklet, or on the website, and check if your scheme offers added years. There will generally be a calculator to show how much it will cost.
>
> Think about whether you can afford to do this, and whether it would benefit you, *before* starting to pay into your scheme's AVC arrangement or any other DC pension.

Financial advisers are required to draw your attention to the existence of any added-years provisions before they sell you another pension, but only you can say how important the security they offer is.

Additional Voluntary Contributions (AVCs)

AVCs can be paid by anyone who is already a member of an employer's pension scheme. They allow you to increase your benefits, provided you do not exceed the current HMRC limits. They are also useful if part of your pay – such as shift premiums or overtime pay – is not counted as pensionable within the employer's scheme. They are defined-contribution (money-purchase) arrangements, so this means that you, not the scheme, carry the risk of the investments not performing as well as you might hope.

> ### ✳ Action Points
>
> Details of the AVC scheme operated by your employer can be obtained from your pensions administrator, trade union representative or personnel officer. They may be included in the scheme booklet or there may be a separate leaflet. Decide whether you can afford to contribute more now towards your retirement income, and if so, whether this would be a good way to do it.

Some schemes operate their own arrangements, but most buy in this facility from one of the major insurance companies or building societies.

In some cases, when you start drawing the pension from the main scheme, your AVCs are used to buy you an extra annuity (explained on pages 237–244) within the scheme. This usually gives you a more favourable rate than if you buy the annuity from the insurance company or on the open market, which are the other alternatives.

Until April 2006, HMRC puts two major restrictions on AVCs. The first is that the maximum contribution by an employee into an AVC and employer's pension scheme combined may not exceed 15 per cent of an employee's total earnings. There is full tax relief on these contributions, given through the PAYE system as with main scheme contributions. The second restriction is that total benefits from an AVC and main pension scheme combined must not exceed the overall benefit limits explained on page 121.

If you do exceed the limits, HMRC insists that the fund returns any excess AVCs plus the investment returns, and this is then taxed. The rates are 32 per cent for basic-rate taxpayers and just under 46 per cent for those paying the higher rate.

Until April 2006, the HMRC rules are that unless you were already paying AVCs before April 1987, the AVC fund must be used to provide a pension and none of it can be commuted into a lump sum. This will change in April 2006 (see page 165).

Some schemes put their own restrictions on how and when you can pay into AVCs, as they are allowed to do under HMRC rules. The scheme may refuse to accept contributions below 0.5 per cent of either your annual taxable earnings or three times the Lower Earnings Limit (currently £82 a week or £4,264 a year), whichever is the higher, in any tax year. Otherwise, you can vary the amounts and timing of your AVCs as much as the scheme allows – but any limits set by the scheme should not be 'unreasonable'. Schemes often allow you to put in an extra lump sum, perhaps from an annual bonus, so long as you remain within the HMRC limits.

Free-Standing Additional Voluntary Contributions (FSAVCs)

FSAVCs are sold by independent providers – insurance companies, building societies and others – rather than being set up and administered within the company. This means that the charges are likely to be considerably higher.

Employees pay contributions net of the basic rate, which is then claimed by the pension provider from HM Revenue & Customs. Higher-rate taxpayers then claim higher-rate relief via the annual tax return.

Until April 2006, there is a 'headroom check' to ensure that the benefits from the main company scheme and an FSAVC taken together do not exceed HMRC limits. This is a calculation done by the FSAVC provider with the co-operation of the main scheme administrator, when FSAVC premiums exceed £200 a month or £2,400 a year.

Currently, everything coming out of the FSAVC has to be taken as pension rather than lump sum, but this will change in 2006.

Stakeholder/personal pensions

Most people in occupational schemes will also be allowed, under the HMRC rules up to April 2006, to pay up to £3,600 a year into a stakeholder (or other personal) pension. If you can afford to do this as well as pay AVCs, you will end up with a higher pension as a result, and can even go above the normal two-thirds limit explained above.

Salary sacrifice

Some employers will allow you to arrange a 'salary sacrifice' in return for higher pension contributions from the employer. This has to follow certain rules to be tax-efficient and should be discussed with your own and the company's accountants. For the employer there can be savings on National Insurance contributions from doing this.

A number of employers have changed the rules of their pension schemes, so that instead of deducting a contribution from your wages, they are now 'non-contributory' and the wages are lower instead, under a salary-sacrifice arrangement. This means that both employer and employee pay lower National Insurance contributions, because the pay from which they are deducted is lower. Some or all of the saving then goes into each individual's pension. However, this can have knock-on effects, especially for the lower-paid, so it is not a good idea for everyone. If your employer is proposing an arrangement of this sort, try to ensure that it is clearly explained and there is full consultation (see page 192 for the new rules on consultation).

Changes from April 2006

With the new tax rules after April 2006, the requirement on schemes to run an AVC scheme will be abolished. However, AVCs are popular with members, and so it seems unlikely that any scheme that already has an AVC arrangement already set up will get rid of it.

More fundamentally, the restrictions on people having a personal/ stakeholder scheme alongside an occupational one will be abolished. So you can then have whatever mix of pensions you want, up to whatever amount you can afford – although you will only get tax relief if you are within the HMRC allowances explained on pages 123–136. FSAVCs will probably die a slow death as a result, because personal and stakeholder pensions are generally more satisfactory products.

You will also be able to take a lump sum, not just a pension, from your AVCs and FSAVCs up to the new AVC limits.

AVCs, FSAVCs or stakeholder pensions?

The in-house AVC is generally likely to be better value than an FSAVC. In many cases, the employer pays the charges which are made by the insurance company or other provider, or will have been able to negotiate a low rate. AVC charges have in any case come down recently, because of competition from stakeholder pensions. There are, however, some poor-quality AVC arrangements around, where the charges and penalties are as steep as if you were buying the policy individually. There are also some where the investment choice is very poor. The scheme trustees should be able to negotiate better terms, and should be pressed on this if they have not done so.

FSAVC charges have also dropped, but they may still be quite high and you could find you are paying commission to those who have sold the policy to you. A rule of thumb is that you could lose around 20 per cent of your contributions, in commission payments and administration, with the average FSAVC. In many, the bulk of these costs will come at the beginning of your policy ('front-end loaded', in the jargon). If you are thinking of taking out an FSAVC to increase your investment choice, consider whether the returns will be so much better that they outweigh these extra costs.

Paying into a stakeholder or personal pension has the following advantages:

- With a stakeholder scheme, the charges are controlled and you cannot be penalised for stopping the pension. However, as pointed out on page 217, the FSA has now allowed the maximum charges for stakeholder pensions to increase, and is planning to relax some of the safeguards, so many people think that there will be increases in both stakeholder and personal pension charges over the coming years.

- If you move jobs, or lose your job, you can carry on paying into the same policy.

For more information, see the FSA's *Guide to Topping Up your Occupational Pension*, which is available free from the FSA at the address on page 262.

✳ Action Points

If you are already paying AVCs or FSAVCs:

- Review your arrangements for buying extra pension, and decide what to do after April 2006.
- Before stopping payments into AVCs or FSAVCs, check whether you will incur any payments by doing so (consult a financial adviser if necessary).
- Find out whether salary sacrifice is on the agenda from your employer, and decide whether it would interest you.
- Consider whether you will want to take a lump sum from your AVCs when you retire.
- Consider whether it is worth moving other investments into your pension fund, to gain the advantage of the tax shelter. It is essential, however, to get independent financial advice before doing this.

Buying extra pension and DC schemes

The limits on contributions up until April 2006 apply to these schemes also, and you have the same choice of AVCs, FSAVCs or personal/stakeholder scheme for your extra money. You may also be able simply to increase your contribution to the main scheme's pension, within limits.

LEAVING AN OCCUPATIONAL SCHEME

If you leave an employer's defined-benefit pension scheme after having been a member for less than two years, you may be able to take a refund of your contributions, depending on the type of scheme. If the scheme is contracted out of S2P, you will receive a refund, but 20 per cent tax will be deducted from it, plus the cost of buying you back into S2P. The two-year period includes any pensionable service transferred from a previous pension scheme, and is a rigid limit. If you go one day over, you lose the right to a refund. Nor is a refund permitted if the fund contains transferred rights from an earlier personal pension policy.

From April 2006 onwards, people who have been members for more than three months but less than two years will have the choice of a refund or a transfer.

For those without the right of refund because they have more than the minimum length of qualifying service, there are several choices:

- If you are 50 (55 from 2010 onwards) or over when you leave, you may be offered an immediate pension, reduced to take into account the longer period over which you will receive it.
- Your pension can be 'deferred' or 'preserved' in the existing scheme (see page 170 for what happens then).
- You have the right to take a transfer. The value of your pension fund can then be transferred to another employer's scheme, if the new trustees allow it, or it can be used to buy a personal pension or a Section 32 'buy-out' bond, as explained below. (See pages 172–175 on how the transfer values of earnings-related pensions are calculated.) There are special rules about the GMP or Protected Rights element of the pension. The trustees of the old scheme are responsible for checking that the policy to which you are transferring meets these.

Section 32 'buy-out' bonds are deferred annuity policies, bought by the trustees from an insurance company chosen by the employee. (An 'annuity' is simply another term for a pension, so a 'deferred annuity' is a pension that is secured for you now but not paid to you until you reach retirement age.) Unlike personal pensions, these deferred annuities will match the benefits originally offered in the employer's scheme, such as a Guaranteed Minimum Pension and provision for spouses.

You have the right to ask for a transfer out of a scheme at any time up to a year before retirement date. However, the new pension scheme may not accept transfers at all, or may allow them only within a certain time limit, especially in the public sector. For example, in the Teachers' Scheme, you can only transfer pension in from elsewhere within a year of starting in the scheme.

There are a few exceptions to the right to take a transfer:

- If the pension dates from a job change before 1986, and has been fully inflation-proofed since then (as it would have been in the public sector, for example), you can be refused a transfer. However, in general, schemes are happy to offer transfers in order to get pensions off their books.
- If the scheme has already been wound up, and your pension rights have been crystallised into an annuity with an insurance company, you cannot then take a transfer. In most cases, however, you will be offered the possibility of taking a transfer at an earlier stage, while winding up is still going on. It will be wise to take independent financial advice about which option is better.
- If your employer is insolvent and your scheme has entered an 'assessment period' for the Pension Protection Fund (see pages 197–198), you will not be able to take a transfer during that period.

Deferred pensions from DB schemes

If you leave a DB scheme before your pension is due, and you decide to leave your pension where it is, the 'deferred' pension you get at retirement will be calculated on the basis of your salary at leaving, multiplied by the accrual rate and by your years of pensionable service. Part of the deferred pension in contracted-out schemes is the Guaranteed Minimum Pension (GMP) built up before April 1997 (explained on page 109). Both this and the remainder of the pension are increased between the date of leaving and the pension date.

Schemes use different formulae for the GMP increases. The most common in the private sector is a fixed annual rate of increase of 4.5 per cent, compounded over the years until you draw the pension (for anyone leaving after April 2002). Public service schemes index-link the GMP. In all cases, if there is a shortfall in the GMP compared with what would have been your SERPS entitlement at retirement, the State makes up the difference. Alternatively, if the GMP is higher than your SERPS entitlement would have been, it stands still for a few years while SERPS catches up.

The remainder of the pension over and above the GMP also increases, either in line with rises in the Retail Prices Index between the time when you leave and the time when you retire or by 5 per cent compounded over those years, whichever is the lower. (Public service schemes are fully index-linked to prices without the 5 per cent ceiling.) This change only came fully into effect in January 1991, so preserved pensions from earlier job changes may have increases on only part of the pension or none at all.

For that part of the pension that builds up after April 1997, there will be no GMP (as explained on page 111). The whole of the post-1997 preserved pension rights will increase over the period of deferment at

5 per cent a year compound or in line with the Retail Prices Index, whichever is the lower.

The effect of revaluation can be seen in the following example (using, for simplicity, a series of contracted-in schemes):

Example

Jim starts working when he is 25 years old. He leaves his first job after ten years and is then earning £10,000 per year. We assume his salary will increase by 5 per cent a year until he retires. He leaves his second job after ten years with a salary of £16,288. At his third job (another ten-year stint) his leaving salary is £26,532, and the final ten-year stretch brings him up to 65 with a leaving salary of £43,219. As can be seen, with revaluation (assuming annual price inflation of 2.5 per cent a year), Jim's pension is increased by around 40 per cent (from £12,004 to £15,603). However, it will not match that earned by people who stay in the same job all their lives, whose whole pension will be based on their final earnings.

	Leaving age	Salary on leaving	After accrual	Preserved pension entitlement	Pension revalued at 2.5% pa
Job 1	35	£10,000	$^{10}/_{80} =$	£1,250	£2,621
Job 2	45	£16,288	$^{10}/_{80} =$	£2,036	£3,336
Job 3	55	£26,532	$^{10}/_{80} =$	£3,316	£4,244
Job 4	65	£43,219	$^{10}/_{80} =$	£5,402	£5,402
			Total	£12,004	£15,603

Total for an employee with 40 continuous years' service =			$^{40}/_{80}$ of	£43,219 =	£21,610

Transfer values

With a DB scheme, the transfer value you take elsewhere represents the cost, calculated by the actuary of your old scheme, of buying the deferred pension (explained above) elsewhere. (An actuary is an expert who calculates risks and their financial implications for life insurance companies and pension schemes.) It will vary depending on your age, interest rates, and the assumptions made by the actuary. Although their professional rules (called Guidance Note 11) have largely standardised the calculations and the minimum level is now laid down by law, actuaries still have a considerable amount of discretion, so transfer values vary considerably between schemes. The actuarial profession is discussing some fairly fundamental changes in their approach to calculating transfer values, which is likely to lead to a considerable increase in their level. The updated Guidance Note (GN11) may come into force in autumn 2005, or may be postponed until 2006.

You may find that once the transfer value has been worked out, it is then reduced by the trustees because the scheme is underfunded. They are allowed to do this. Indeed, if there is a hole in the scheme's finances, it is only fair that they do so because otherwise those who leave the scheme will take more than their share of the 'pot' and those who stay will be penalised. The trustees have to tell you what the reduction is, and also estimate the date when it will be possible to return to full transfer values, so that you have the choice of whether to move your pension now, or wait until the funding builds up again.

✽ Action Points

If your deferred pension would be large and you are dissatisfied with the amount of the transfer payment, consider bringing in another pensions professional – probably another actuary – to negotiate on your behalf. This can often be successful, but you will need to pay a fee for the assistance. You can find an actuary through the Association of Consulting Actuaries (address on page 265).

If you think there has been maladministration, or if there is a dispute over the facts that have been used in the calculation, you can also go to the Pensions Advisory Service (address on page 264) or the Pensions Ombudsman (address on page 264) after raising the issue with the scheme's trustees through the internal disputes procedure, explained on page 199.

If you are offered a reduced transfer value, consider very carefully what to do in this situation. If a scheme started winding up before 6 April 2005 and there is not enough money to go round, the pensioners have priority for what there is. Current and deferred members may find a considerable shortfall. For schemes that started winding up after that date, the priority is to cover the liabilities that would be met by the Pension Protection Fund (see pages 197–198). If the employer is insolvent, then the PPF takes responsibility for these 'protected liabilities'. If not, then the employer must meet the full buy-out costs for them – that means the full cost of buying annuities or deferred annuities from an insurance company. Ask your trade union, or a Citizens Advice Bureau, for advice.

What a transfer buys

In some cases, transferring into a new employer's scheme can buy you extra periods of service within that scheme. In the main public services, for example, there is a 'transfer club' which means that you are given credits according to a standard table used by each scheme. In some cases this will be year for year – in other words, if you have ten years' service in the last one, you will be counted as having ten years' service in the new scheme. In other cases, the schemes are different; a year's service in one may be counted as rather more, or rather less, than a year in another scheme. In the Teachers' Scheme, for example, the normal retirement age is currently 60, which means that a pension in it is more valuable than one in the Local Government Pension Scheme (LGPS), where it is 65. So someone transferring from the LGPS to the Teachers' Scheme will receive slightly less than a full year's credited service for each year they transfer.

There are time limits on being able to make use of the transfer club. If you miss these and transfer later, you will be offered a much lower amount of credited service. So it is important to keep within the deadlines.

Example

Elsa works for the NHS and builds up 8½ years' service in their scheme. She then goes to work for a local authority and joins their pension scheme. She can bring her 8½ years' credits with her.

In the private sector, however, there is no transfer club. You may be offered extra years' service in your new employer's scheme, but they will often be fewer years' service than in the previous scheme. This is partly because the benefits in the two schemes will be different. The main reason, however, is that it is expected that your earnings will rise, on average, faster than has been allowed for in the transfer-value calculations. You may be offered a DC pension for this element in your new scheme, rather than a pension linked to your earnings.

If you make a transfer into a stakeholder or personal pension or a Section 32 buy-out bond, it will certainly become a money-purchase benefit.

Leaving a DC scheme

If yours is a contracted-out money-purchase (COMP) scheme, you will not be able to have a refund, but only a preserved or transferred pension.

If you decide to leave your pension where it is, rather than transfer, the pension will be made 'paid-up', with the charges that have built up so far deducted at this stage. How much these are varies between schemes. With the less good ones, they are quite high and could eat up much of the fund that has built up so far. With the best, there may be no deductions at all. Your pension account then continues to receive the same investment returns as that of any other member, but there will be no further payments into it from either your employer or yourself. The actual pension you get at retirement will be affected by interest rates in force at the time.

If you take a transfer, it is simply the value of the accumulated fund, after any deductions, that is transferred.

What should you do?

It is impossible to give definite advice in a book like this, as so much depends on individual circumstances, but here are a few rules of thumb:

- Be very cautious about taking a transfer of a deferred pension from a DB scheme into a personal pension. You will be swapping a benefit that is guaranteed (although only to the extent of the PPF-protected liabilities – see pages 197–198 if the employer becomes insolvent) for an uncertain one, and also in general paying substantial charges to the company that administers the personal pension (and commission to the person who sells it to you).

- If your scheme is index-linked, for example if it is a public service scheme, it is even less likely to be wise to transfer into a personal pension scheme.
- It is sometimes sensible to take a transfer across from one DB scheme to another. It all depends on the terms offered and your prospects in the new job. If the new employer is keen for you to take the job, you may be able to bargain for added years in the new scheme. In the public sector, the transfer club makes it much easier – but there are deadlines, so make sure you keep to them.
- It *may* be sensible to transfer between DC schemes, or from a DC scheme to a personal pension. Again, it depends on the terms offered and the charges.

In 1993–1994, a major scandal relating to pension transfers was revealed in the financial world. It was estimated that up to half a million people had been 'mis-sold' personal pension transfers when they would have done better to leave their deferred pensions with the old employer.

As a result, the Financial Services Authority (FSA) now has tight rules governing those selling pension transfer policies. Before a sale is finalised, you must be sent a 'reasons why' letter explaining precisely why they think that buying a new policy with your transfer value is the right course for you. They should also do a 'transfer value analysis' to show what rate of return you would need in order to benefit. Do not proceed with a transfer without such a letter and analysis, and then only if you feel the reasons are particularly strong.

Whatever you do with the transfer value of your pension, it need not affect your pension choices with your new employer. You could buy a single-premium personal pension policy with it and then start afresh in a new company pension scheme. After April 2006, if you can afford it you can continue to pay into the personal pension as well.

For more information, see the FSA's *Guide to the Risks of Pension Transfers,* available free from the FSA at the address on page 262.

Pensions 'liberation' – warning

The official bodies concerned with pensions have issued warnings about a new scam which is tempting people who would like to get hold of money from their pension funds. People calling themselves financial advisers offer to turn pension benefits into a tax-free lump sum immediately. They then ask the individual's existing pension scheme to transfer their pension money to a new scheme, which may well be in the name of a fictitious employer.

These 'liberators' usually charge high commissions, ranging from 20 to 30 per cent of the individual's total fund. On top of this, people could find that they have a tax bill. Someone in the higher tax bracket could pay up to 30 per cent of their fund in commission to the pension 'liberator' and then be liable to pay 40 per cent tax on the whole amount including the commission. That would mean losing in the region of 70 per cent of their total fund. (There have been cases where the 'liberators' have simply disappeared with the money. Two have recently been prosecuted.)

If trustees have suspicions regarding the scheme requesting a transfer payment, they can refuse to pay, and tell the requesting scheme to write to the Pensions Regulator if they are not happy.

HM Revenue & Customs also now says that cheques for transfer payments must not, in any circumstances, be made payable to independent financial advisers or brokers. If the receiving scheme is a:

- personal pension, or an insured occupational scheme, then the cheque must be made payable to the insurance company;
- small self-administered scheme (SSAS, as explained on pages 145–146), then the trustees must get written confirmation that all

is above board, and that the money will go into a bank account where the professional trustee is a co-signatory; or

- large self-administered scheme, then the trustees must ask them to authorise HM Revenue & Customs to confirm whether the scheme is properly approved for tax purposes or not.

For more information, see Revenue SPSS Update 132, *Improper Transfers: Trust Busting,* which is available on the Internet at www.hmrc.gov.uk, and also the FSA's *Unlocking Pensions: Make Sure You Understand the Risks,* which is available at www.fsa.gov.uk/consumer/pdfs/unlock_pension.pdf

---

✱ Action Points

When you leave a job:

- Check the possibilities of a transfer to the new scheme, if you are eligible for it. You may want to get financial advice on whether it is worthwhile or not.
- Ask whether there is a deadline on transferring on favourable terms, and be careful to keep within it if so.
- Don't be tempted by a 'pensions liberation' scam, and if someone approaches you with one, report them to the Pensions Regulator (address on page 264).

If your employer changes

Over the past few years, many people have found that their job has remained the same but the employer has changed, perhaps because of a takeover or because of the contracting out of services in the public sector.

The legal position here is quite complex, because pensions do not have the same protection as other conditions of employment under the Transfer of Undertakings (Protection of Employment) Regulations (usually called TUPE). On the other hand, there may be alternative contractual protection. In a few cases, such as local government and teaching, a new employer may be able to arrange for you to stay with the existing scheme. There are also a few schemes which cover more than one employer in the same industry – such as the Railways Pension Scheme for those working for the different railway companies. So far as their own staff and those in other parts of the public sector are concerned, there have been directives from the Government about treatment of pensions when work is transferred to private contractors. This means that normally public sector workers' pensions, both past and future, are well protected. There have also been some European Court cases that suggest that pension entitlement on redundancy or early retirement (other than due to ill-health) may transfer over to a new employer under TUPE, especially in public–private transfers. However, the lawyers seem undecided about the impact of these cases. Contact your union or Citizens Advice Bureau if you think this might be relevant to you.

For those in other schemes, under *The Pensions Act 2004* there is some new but fairly limited protection under TUPE for people whose employers are taken over after April 2005. Broadly, if the former employer in a business transfer provided access to a defined-benefit or defined-contribution scheme; and, in a money-purchase scheme, made contributions of more than the minimum contracted-out rebate (explained on page 108), then the employer has three options:

- provide a replacement defined-benefit structure at least equivalent to that required to contract out – that is, the fairly modest Reference Scheme explained on page 111;
- provide a replacement defined-contribution scheme with matching contributions up to a ceiling, which will probably be 6 per cent; or
- contribute at the same rate to a stakeholder arrangement of which the employee is, or could be, a member.

Employers are not very likely to offer the first alternative unless they are required to by the vendor, because the others are much less of a burden on them. Some large companies do make it a condition of sale, when they are divesting themselves of unwanted subsidiaries, that the new employer provides equivalent benefits. If you are part of a group of specialist staff, so that the value of the business will disappear if you walk away, you may also be in a strong bargaining position to get a replacement scheme modelled on, or comparable with, the previous one. If you are a member of a trade union or staff association, it should be able to assist with negotiating on the new package.

Even if the new provision is not as good as the previous one, it will almost always be worth joining the new scheme for future service (see page 146). Whether you should transfer your previous scheme benefits for the years you were a member there, is much more doubtful. If the new employer is financially secure, and you are offered year-for-year credits or something comparable, it could be worth transferring. If you are not sure of the new employer's viability, or think your own job might disappear rather quickly, you probably should not. You should also be very cautious about transferring from a final-salary scheme to a money-purchase one. Much depends on your age, your earnings, how good the old scheme is and what the new one offers. Press for the new employer to arrange individual financial counselling, as there is too much variation for blanket advice to be useful.

It is only possible for an employer to make a 'bulk transfer' without the members' consent if the actuary will certify that the members will receive past service benefits in the new scheme as good as those they are giving up. This is less strong protection than it looks, because the question is whether, if the scheme to which they are being transferred winds up, they will get less than they would have had if the previous scheme wound up. However, actuaries are wary of committing themselves on this and so bulk transfers without consent are rare.

Change of employer and DC schemes

The new rules explained above also cover defined-contribution schemes, provided that the employer is contributing more than just the National Insurance rebates.

If the company is being reorganised

There are some extra considerations if the transfer of employment is between subsidiaries in the same company group – perhaps because the company is moving all the staff's contracts to a service company with no assets. *The Pensions Act 2004* includes some very extensive powers for the Regulator to require other parts of a company group to make contributions or give financial support to a pension scheme in one part, if it considers that the rearrangement is in order to avoid paying a deficit on the scheme. There are requirements for the trustees and advisers to notify the Regulator of details of any such company arrangement.

✳ Action Points

If you think that the Regulator has not been notified, contact your trade union or Public Concern at Work (address on page 267) to give them the information, rather than do it yourself. Although the Regulator would try to protect your anonymity, it would not be able to guarantee this and you could be putting your own future at risk.

EARLY RETIREMENT

How much you can get on early retirement under an employer's pension scheme varies enormously. Unless the retirement is due to ill-health (see below), you will not in any case be able to draw the employer's pension before you are 50 (55 from 2010 onwards). It will then be worked out taking into account the number of years you have been a member of the scheme and your earnings at retirement, or the size of the fund available in a money-purchase scheme. If you are taking early retirement at the employer's request or if you are suffering from ill-health, you may be given credits for some or all of your prospective years of service (the period up to retirement when you could have worked but are not going to).

Especially if you are retiring at your own request, you may find that the early retirement pension is very small. It could be reduced well below its normal amount, because of an 'actuarial reduction'. This is designed to spread the same amount of pension over a longer period. The figures used vary; the reduction could be 6 per cent for each year of early retirement, for example.

Example

Ahmed decides to retire at 60. His scheme has a retirement age of 65, but his pension is calculated only on the years of service he has actually worked, up to 60. It is then reduced by 30 per cent; in other words, 6 per cent for each year that he could have worked, if he had carried on to the company's normal retirement age.

At worst, you may not be allowed to draw a pension at all, if most of it consists of Guaranteed Minimum Pension (GMP: explained on page 109). This is because the law says that there must be enough in the scheme to pay the proper GMP entitlement when you reach retirement age. If you are paid some pension early, there might not be enough. So in some schemes, the whole pension is held back to make sure.

On the other hand, a better employer should be willing to add to your pension so that there is enough in the fund for you to draw some pension early without harming the later GMP. Check your scheme booklet to see what is on offer. If it does not seem very good, ask your union or staff association to try to negotiate a better deal.

You may find that there are restrictions on taking other employment once you have started drawing the pension, especially in the public sector (see pages 187–188).

Final-salary schemes can be very flexible over early retirement, especially if there is a surplus on the fund which means that extra money for a particular case can be found without harming the rest. However, early retirements can be very expensive, because it means less has come in as contributions and the pension will be paid for a longer time than if you worked on to normal retirement date. So many schemes, especially in the public sector, have tightened up the rules on early retirement considerably. Particularly if your scheme is running a deficit, you may find that it is not allowing early retirements where it would have done a few years ago, or is only allowing them if the employer puts in an extra lump-sum contribution to cover the (substantial) extra cost.

Early retirement and DC schemes

In general, your pension from a DC scheme is simply the annuity that your individual 'pot' of money will buy at any time. If you are taking early retirement, you can expect your pension to be paid for much longer, so the same amount of money has to be spread out further. So the 'actuarial reductions' in a DC scheme tend to be very heavy for anyone retiring early, whatever the reason.

If you are retiring at the employer's request, you may be able to persuade them to put an extra lump sum into your DC account, so that the pension can be bigger.

To help people with long-term sickness or disability, some employers with DC schemes have an 'income protection' or 'permanent health insurance' arrangement. This is usually provided by an insurance policy, separately from the pension scheme (although the same people within the company may be responsible for it). Details of what is available should be included in your staff handbook or your employment contract.

✶ Action Points

If you are thinking of taking early retirement, look at your scheme booklet or website to see what is available in your particular scheme. If there is a calculator available on the website, you should be able to establish what it would mean for you. Remember that any reduction for early retirement is permanent, however long you live, and cost-of-living increases will almost certainly also be given on the reduced sum, not on the original pension. Check the impact on your spouse's pension too.

Insist on a statement in writing of what you will get before committing yourself to early retirement.

If you are paying Additional Voluntary Contributions or have a personal or stakeholder pension, check how those will be reduced if you start to draw them early. The reductions may be considerable, so calculate whether you can afford to live without drawing them, at least for a while.

If you have worked for other employers in the past, and have left deferred pensions with them, you may also be able to ask for them to be paid early. However, they will probably be heavily reduced. Ask the trustees of your former schemes for details of what you would get, and of what their policy is.

If you are taking severance or being made redundant, it may be possible for you to arrange for a lump sum to go into the pension scheme from your employer, to increase your pension, with an equivalent cut in a severance or redundancy payment. Ask the pensions administrator or HR department if this could be arranged.

Ill-health retirement

If you are too sick to work, then you will usually need to apply to the trustees of the scheme for ill-health retirement. In some schemes, however, it is the employer who takes the decision and tells the trustees what to do. Whoever takes the decision should do so after taking proper medical advice. Much depends on the precise wording of the rule in your scheme. In particular, does it say that you have to be incapable of doing *any* job before you can receive a pension, or is it enough to be incapable of doing your *own* job or a similar one? And does it say that you must be *permanently* incapable?

The Pensions Ombudsman has had to deal with a number of cases about ill-health retirement, and some broad rules about how early retirements should be treated can be taken from his rulings:

- You will need to co-operate with the pensions administrators and trustees, for example in going for a medical examination with a consultant, and giving consent for the relevant people to see your medical records. However, if the demands being made on you are unreasonable given your condition, explain this in writing and say what you think would be reasonable.
- The trustees or employer should let you know the reasons for any rejection, so that you can challenge them if they have any of the facts wrong.
- If your condition would be improved by an operation or a course of treatment that it is reasonable to expect you to undertake, you would probably be refused early retirement until you had done so. However, if it was a risky operation without much chance of success, you should not be expected to go through with it as a condition of getting the pension.

Terminal illness

Many scheme rules say that, if someone is terminally ill, the whole of the pension can be commuted into a lump sum, although some tax will be paid on it.

✳ Action Points

If you are thinking of asking for ill-health retirement, check the scheme rules (see page 201 for your rights to information) and the procedure that is undertaken.

If you feel your case is not clear-cut, it could be wise to ask TPAS (see page 264) for advice and to discuss the question with your union before you start the application.

If you think you have not been fairly treated, check the procedures and definitions of 'ill-health' (it might be called 'invalidity' or 'incapacity' in your scheme) laid down in the trust deed. Every scheme has to have an internal disputes procedure (explained on page 199), so if you are dissatisfied you should take your case through that, if necessary with the help of TPAS.

WORKING AFTER RETIREMENT AGE

If you work beyond your pension scheme's normal retirement age (NRA), many occupational pension schemes provide for you to build up extra pension entitlement by postponing the start of your pension.

With a contracted-out salary-related (COSR) scheme, if you put off drawing your pension for at least seven complete weeks after State Pension age, your Guaranteed Minimum Pension will increase. The amount that earnings-related occupational schemes provide over and above the GMP for late retirement can vary; check your scheme booklet. (The new rules for State pensions, explained on page 75, do not apply to GMPs.)

Working after retirement age and DC schemes

In a contracted-out money-purchase (COMP) scheme, deferring drawing the pension should mean that the Protected Rights benefit will be increased. The whole pension fund in any kind of money-purchase scheme may continue to grow in value during the extra time you stay at work. However, there is always the danger that the investment market may continue to stagnate or even fall – perhaps dramatically – so that the value of your fund therefore also declines. Until April 2006, you cannot draw your occupational pension and continue to work for the *same* employer, although there is nothing in the rules to stop you going to work for another one. Once HMRC's tax reforms come in (as outlined on pages 123–136), they will allow you to continue working while drawing all or part of your pension from that employer. However, employers will not be compelled to change their own pension schemes' rules to allow this, and it may take quite some time before they do so.

Public sector schemes

The main public sector schemes have what are called 'abatement' rules. This means that if you as a scheme member take a pension and then continue to work in a job covered by the same scheme (for example, for another local council if you are an LGPS pensioner), your pension is reduced or cut altogether. The idea is that your pension plus pay in the new job must be restricted to the same level as your earnings when you left the old job (plus inflation). The rules are really intended to catch senior people manipulating the position, but they affect many more people than that and are highly unpopular. They also seem to go against the Government's ideas on flexible retirement, so they may be abolished within the next few years, or modified.

Age discrimination rules

From September 2006 onwards, there will be a new law forbidding 'unjustified' discrimination against people on grounds of their age. Employers will still be able to require people to retire at the age of 65, but employees will have the 'right to request' that they stay on.

There will also be an effect on the rules of many pension schemes, but we will not know exactly what that is until the regulations are finalised.

✳ Action Points

Check the late retirement rules and in particular whether there is any penalty.

Take financial advice if you think you may not start to draw the annuity at retirement age. You may find you do better to start drawing it while still working, and invest the proceeds if you do not need them to live on.

Think about whether you might want to increase your pension by continuing to work for the same employer (perhaps part-time) after your scheme's NRA.

Check how the pension will increase if you do, and what your employer's attitude would be to the idea.

If you are thinking of working on, but with another employer, check how the deferred pension increases if you postpone taking it beyond NRA.

If you belong to one of the public sector schemes:

- check the position in your scheme if you are planning to retire but continue to work in another job in the public sector; and
- if necessary, alter your ideas about what job to get. The 'abatement' rules do not affect you if your new job is with another part of the public sector (for example, the NHS if you are an LGPS pensioner) or in the private sector.

HOW SECURE IS YOUR OCCUPATIONAL PENSION?

Most defined-benefit pension schemes, most of the time, are fairly secure and provide the benefits that their members expect without any problems. However, the Maxwell scandal, and a few others during the recession of the early 1990s, made many people feel far less secure about their pensions than they did in the past. More recently, with the fall in the stock market and changes in the rules for accounting for pensions, we have seen many press stories about 'deficits' or 'black holes' in final-salary schemes. So this section looks at two different aspects: whether your scheme is being properly administered; and whether it has the funds to pay the benefits that have been promised.

Is your scheme being properly run?

The vast majority of pension schemes do appear to be well run and properly safeguarded. The number of scandals that have arisen is really very small as a proportion of the number of schemes in existence (although, of course, there should not be any at all). The protection for scheme members at present lies with:

- the trustees;
- the scheme's auditor and actuary;
- the new Pensions Regulator, which started in April 2005; and
- the Pensions Advisory Service (TPAS), the Pensions Ombudsman and the courts.

Is there enough money to meet the promises?

During the 1980s and much of the 1990s things were going very well for occupational pension schemes and they were very cheap to run.

Costs are now rising and employers are becoming increasingly reluctant to pay what is needed.

Until 1997, it was left to the employer, the actuary and the trustees to sort out together how much money was needed to go into the funds to meet the promise that the employer had made. In 1997 a minimum standard was set (under *The Pensions Act 1995*) called the Minimum Funding Requirement or MFR. To be comfortable, a scheme should be financed at well above that level, but unfortunately many employers assumed that the 'minimum' was the 'standard', and funded only at that level, so that when the stock market fell from 2000 onwards, they found that there was not enough money to meet the promises they had made. These had anyway become more expensive, partly because of legal changes and partly because people are living longer.

A new set of rules will come into force in October 2005 and will require trustees to set their own 'scheme-specific' funding standards. Perhaps more importantly, the law was changed in 2004 to say that if a pension scheme is wound up, the full cost of 'buying out' the pensions becomes a debt on the employer. If the employer is insolvent and cannot pay this, the new Pension Protection Fund (explained on pages 197–198) will provide some (but not complete) compensation for scheme members' loss.

What should you do if your scheme is closed?

First of all, clarify what is happening. It can mean:

- not allowing any new employees to join, but letting existing members continue to build up rights (although they are usually offered the chance to transfer to any new arrangement that is being set up);

- closing it for new starters, and also stopping existing members building up any more pension rights for future service. When someone retires, their pension might be calculated on their salary at retirement, but without their later years of service being included. More usually today, however, it will be calculated on the salary at the date the scheme closed and then given the statutory increases just as if the members had left service. People are usually offered the chance to join the new arrangement, if one is being set up, and to transfer the value of their accumulated pension into it; or
- closing it down altogether, so that people have the choice of transferring, having a 'bought out' deferred pension, or buying their own personal/stakeholder pension.

If it is the first, then as an existing member your pension prospects will not be damaged. In the short term, however, the scheme may then become a 'dinosaur', and ensuring that it is properly run and protected against future closure may become increasingly difficult. If it is either of the other two alternatives, your prospects will be damaged and you will have some decisions to take. Usually, any new arrangement offered will be a defined-contribution scheme (explained on pages 98–100), which is often inferior. As explained on pages 175–177, you should be very cautious about transferring a pension that has already built up between a defined-benefit and a defined-contribution scheme – seek advice before doing so.

In some cases, employers who have announced plans to close their schemes have been persuaded to reconsider through the pressure brought to bear by employees. There have usually been some concessions by the employees, however, such as:

- agreeing to have the pension build up at a lower rate for the future;
- agreeing to pay a higher contribution; or
- losing rights to retire early on favourable terms.

Consultation about changes or closure

Most public sector schemes already include an obligation on the Government to consult about changes. There are also long-standing obligations to consult before changing the contracting-out decision for the scheme. For other elements of private sector pension schemes, *The Pensions Act 2004* includes new requirements for employers to consult unions, or other representatives, before they change benefits for the future. These apply to both defined-benefit and defined-contribution schemes.

There are also wider obligations on employers to consult, in line with a new European Union law, the *Information and Consultation Directive*.

Essentially, the new requirements are that employers must consult the trade unions or other representatives on major changes to future pension arrangements, and that trustees may not decide on such changes without first notifying the employer, and subsequently satisfying themselves that the employer has consulted as required. The Regulator can waive or relax these rules in specific cases. The failure to comply will not affect the validity of any trustees' decisions.

There are time limits on the process, and protection of employee representatives against detriment or dismissal by employers. The detailed regulations prescribe what information must be provided, make rules about how employee representatives are to be selected, and require or authorise the holding of ballots.

The changes to occupational schemes that will be covered by the new law are:

- increasing the age at which the pension becomes payable;
- closing the scheme to new members;

- closing the scheme to the accrual of further benefits;
- ending an employer's liability to pay contributions;
- introducing members' contributions where there were none before;
- changing a defined-benefit scheme to a defined-contribution scheme;
- reducing the rate of future benefit accrual;
- increasing members' contributions by more than 2 per cent; and
- for defined-contribution schemes, reducing employer contributions by more than 2 per cent, or to bring them below 3 per cent.

What often happens is that an employer offers a 'choice' (though rather a forced one) of continuing at the same level with a low accrual rate, or making higher payments to keep the same rate. A few employers have been tougher and said that anyone who does not accept the change will have to leave the scheme and become a deferred member.

Changing past benefits

There are tighter restrictions – not surprisingly – on the employer's power to alter retrospectively the benefits you have already built up. Under *The Pensions Act 2004,* from April 2006, schemes are able to make rule changes that affect any entitlements or 'accrued rights' of the members only if:

- there is a power in the scheme rules to make the change;
- the change does not involve converting defined-benefit rights into defined-contribution rights;
- the trustees approve the change;
- the total actuarial value of members' accrued rights at the point of any change is maintained;

- pensions already in payment are not reduced; and
- members are consulted before a change is made.

For any amendments that do *not* meet these tests, before making them the trustees have to satisfy themselves that either:

- an actuary has given a certificate that the amendment is not detrimental; or
- the members' consent has been obtained.

Trustees are then not allowed to impose a detrimental amendment on an individual member from whom they have not heard.

If a pension scheme is being wound up

If the employer is going out of business, this will usually trigger the start of a wind-up process for the pension scheme. An employer who is staying in business is also generally able to insist that a scheme is wound up, by giving notice to the trustees or by refusing to pay the right contributions so that the trustees themselves must start the process.

If the scheme is contracted-out of S2P/SERPS (explained on pages 107–114), the employer must inform the members, by giving them a 'notice of intention', and consult the recognised trade unions.

The scheme's trustees then have to distribute any assets that still remain, following the rules laid down in the trust deed. They can do this by transferring them to another scheme, or by taking out insurance policies – immediate annuities for the pensioners and deferred annuities for everyone else. The members cannot, however, get a cash payout, as the money set aside for their pensions must always go into some other pension arrangement.

For a final-salary scheme, even if the scheme is well-funded on an ongoing basis, there can be a shortfall when it is winding up, because the annuities that have to be bought are expensive and the scheme may not be able to realise its investments at the value it has placed on them. Most will therefore have a deficit on a winding-up.

A shortfall in funding becomes a debt on the employer. For schemes which begin winding up on or after 11 June 2003, if the employer is still solvent, then they will need to meet the full cost of buying out pensions, *unless* they can convince the trustees that to do so will push them into insolvency. In the past, some employers and trustees have reached 'compromise agreements' reducing the debt. Since April 2005, these have had to be reported to the Pensions Regulator, who has power to intervene if the trustees have not been tough enough with the employer. If you hear of a compromise agreement being reached in your scheme, try to find out whether the Regulator has been consulted, and what attitude they took. However, the debt is only an ordinary unsecured one. Debts to the banks will probably have been secured on the buildings and property, leaving little over for any other debtor.

✳ Action Points

If the employer is proposing to change or close your pension scheme:

- Ask whether they are complying with the consultation regulations, and stress that 'consultation' has been defined by Employment Tribunals as meaning that there should be room for a change of mind after hearing other arguments, rather than simply presentation of something that has already been decided. Even if you are not unionised, there is still a requirement under the regulations to consult with employee representatives.
- If you belong to a trade union, ask for its assistance in weighing up the proposals and if necessary fighting against them.
- If you are not unionised, you may want to discuss the plans with TPAS, at least to check that the employer understands and is following its legal obligations.

If the shortfall was caused by 'fraud or misappropriation' (but not just because the investments have done badly), the Pensions Protection Fund (PPF) has a separate section which can pay individuals' benefits while the scheme is sorted out, and then pay over a lump sum to wind up the scheme. No one needs to have been convicted of fraud for the PPF to take action under this, but the requirements before it can take on a case are tight.

Winding up a scheme can take several years. The Government has brought in regulations, from April 2002, to try to speed things up. The new law is being phased in to apply first to those schemes that have been winding up the longest. There must be regular reports to the Pensions Regulator about what is happening, and information to scheme members.

Winding up a DC scheme

In a defined-contribution scheme, the amount available is simply the value of each person's pension 'pot', less the deduction of the expenses of winding up (which can be considerable). The trustees will buy deferred annuities with these, and if the pensions are contracted out, these will include cover for the Protected Rights (explained on page 112).

If the company is insolvent

If the company has a final-salary scheme, and there is no-one independent on the trustee board, the Regulator may appoint a special Independent Trustee (IT). (It does not have to, however, if this would just increase the expense unnecessarily and where the existing trustees can do the job.) This IT then takes over the powers of the trustee board, and does the work needed to wind up the scheme.

In due course, the former members should be sent individual notification of their benefits, and the name of the insurance company with which they have been bought. Statements showing the value of each person's pension benefits must be provided on request within two months to any member who asks for one.

Only when all the queries raised by this process have been resolved will the scheme be completely wound up.

Many insolvent companies are given permission to continue trading, and parts are sold off as going concerns. It may be possible to persuade the new employer to continue the scheme or to set up a new one with the same arrangements. This called a 'scheme rescue' under *The Pensions Act 2004*.

The Pension Protection Fund

From April 2005, there is a new Pension Protection Fund (PPF), which is intended to provide compensation if the employer is insolvent and there is a deficit on the fund which means that full pensions cannot be paid. It does not, however, cover the full amount of the loss. Instead, it will give:

- 100 per cent of the pensions currently being paid for pensioners over retirement age and those retired because of ill-health;
- 90 per cent of the accrued entitlement for early-retired members, deferred pensioners and active members; and
- pension increases only of 2.5 per cent per year, and only on the pension built up since 1997.

Spouses' and dependants' pensions will also be paid, but according to the PPF's own rules rather than the scheme's rules. There is also a ceiling on the amount of pension that can be paid to any one individual. The PPF will take over the funds of the insolvent companies' pension schemes it accepts under its wing, and run them itself. In addition, it will impose a levy on all defined-benefit schemes in the private sector.

For those whose schemes have already collapsed and left a shortfall before April 2005, there is a much more limited Financial Assistance Scheme. Eligible workers who were within three years of their scheme's pension age on 14 May 2004 will receive 80 per cent of their core promised benefits, but without any future increases, and only once their scheme has actually been wound up. The Government has said it will review the position after three years.

For more information, see *An Introductory Guide to the Pension Protection Fund*, available online at www.pensionprotectionfund.org.uk or by phoning 020 8867 3297, and also *An Introduction to the Pensions Regulator,* available online at www.thepensionsregulator.gov.uk or by phoning 0870 606 3636.

Pension scheme contributions

Legally, employees' contributions have to be passed on to the fund by the 19th of the month after which they were deducted (the same date as for tax and NI payments). If your company becomes insolvent and has failed to hand over employees' payments to the pension fund in the previous 12 months, trustees can make a claim on the Government's Redundancy Fund. The claim cannot total more than 10 per cent of the employees' pay or the amount certified by the actuary as the shortfall in the fund, whichever is the lower. In theory, if the scheme is contracted out, HM Revenue & Customs can also in some cases 'deem' NI contributions to have been paid and reinstate people in S2P, but this has not yet happened satisfactorily in more than a handful of cases. Any remaining shortfall is a debt on the insolvent company.

✳ Action Points

If your company pension scheme runs into problems, get help from your union or TPAS to help you through the legal technicalities.

Compensation and DC schemes

If the employer wants to change or close down the scheme, the requirements on consultation explained on pages 192–197 apply in the same way as for a DB scheme.

If your scheme is closed down, the value of your pot of pension, less any charges, will be used to set up a deferred pension (as if you had left) or to buy an annuity, depending on your age. You may also be able to take a transfer elsewhere.

Because there is no promise of a particular level of pension, defined-contribution schemes are not covered by the main Pension Protection Fund. However, if the fund is lost because of fraud or theft, the PPF may provide compensation to cover the loss, from the separate section held for this purpose. The Pensions Regulator supervises DC as well as DB schemes.

Complaints and disputes about your scheme

Under *The Pensions Act 1995*, every scheme (of either sort) has to have a formal 'internal disputes procedure' for scheme members and potential members. To start this procedure, you write to a 'nominated person' (usually the pension manager) about your grievance. This person must reply within two months. If you are still not satisfied, you can go to the trustees (or, in a public service scheme, the relevant authorities). The rules for this are to be simplified from September 2005, to allow schemes to have only one rather than two stages.

After that, if you still are not satisfied, there is the Pensions Advisory Service (TPAS) and the Pensions Ombudsman. TPAS is a voluntary body drawing on the good offices of retired and active pensions professionals around the country. It will give advice and take up grievances; it can be contacted directly or via a Citizens Advice Bureau. If you feel that your dispute is especially complex, you may like to ask TPAS to help you go through the disputes procedure.

Many of the cases TPAS deals with are simply the result of misunderstanding and poor administration; these can be cleared up fairly quickly. Those problems it cannot solve are referred to the Pensions Ombudsman for investigation. The Ombudsman can deal with questions of maladministration, or disputes over fact or law, and has the power to enforce decisions through the courts.

However, employers and trustees can appeal against the Pensions Ombudsman's decisions in the courts. If they do, then usually the person who has complained to the Ombudsman, and the Ombudsman himself, are not represented because the cost will be too high, and so there is a danger that their side of the case is not heard. The courts have also imposed a number of limits on the powers of the Ombudsman to hear cases and to order redress, making him less effective than was originally intended.

The alternative route with a grievance is to go to court. But this is a slow and cumbersome procedure, and there is also the risk of high costs. It is sometimes possible for scheme members to get a court order that the fund should pay the costs, but there is always the risk that the court will not agree to it. This is one reason why the Pensions Ombudsman was first set up.

Employment Tribunals also play some role in pensions, especially where there is an issue of unfair dismissal or discrimination on grounds of race or sex. They are much cheaper to deal with than courts, although they can still be very legalistic.

The new Pensions Regulator

From April 2005 there is a new 'proactive' Pensions Regulator (tPR). This replaces the previous one, Opra, which had limited powers and had to wait until it was told about things going wrong. The Regulator's role will be to concentrate on areas where members are at greatest risk from breaches, and be proactive in analysing risks. Its key objective is to reduce the risks of claims on the PPF (explained on pages 197–198). It will also provide education, advice and guidance, and be required to take account of the interests of the members. It will work on the basis of issuing Codes of Practice, which employers and trustees will be encouraged, but not required, to follow. It will be able to punish those who do not follow the law, and to give them instructions about how to run their schemes better.

For more information, see the Pensions Regulator's booklets and website (address on page 264).

Getting information

You have a legal right to information about your occupational pension scheme. Most of the basic facts will be in the scheme booklet, but you will also find useful material in the annual report. In most cases, the full report is not sent out to members automatically, but often a short version is, or a notice is put on the staff notice-board or the intranet. You have a right to request the full document, which should explain what the scheme's activities have been over the last year, how the money has been invested, and what benefits are being paid out. There should also be a contact address for further queries.

You also have a right to see the legal documents covering the scheme, which are:

- the trust deed;
- the Statement of Investment Principles; and
- the actuarial valuation (for defined-benefit schemes), and in due course a new Statement of Funding Principles.

So far as your own benefits are concerned, you have a right to a written statement of these if you ask for it, provided that you have not already received one within the last 12 months. In practice, most schemes provide statements automatically every year. You also have the right to know what the transfer value (explained on pages 172–177) would be if you left the scheme.

✳ Action Points

For information about the scheme, ask for copies of the relevant scheme documents and go through them.

For further queries, write to the administrator or secretary of the pension scheme.

If the information you request is not given to you, complain to the Pensions Regulator.

If you have concerns about the scheme, you might also want to ask that the scheme administrator or one of the trustees come to a workplace meeting where those concerns can be discussed.

PERSONAL AND STAKEHOLDER PENSIONS

Personal pensions (including stakeholder pensions, which are a special type of personal pension) are all defined-contribution arrangements. Each person has an individual contract with the insurance company or another provider, even if the employer helps with setting up the contracts and makes a contribution.

This chapter looks at the different types of arrangement, how you buy a personal pension, what happens if you want to stop paying in or if you want to increase your pension, and what special issues women should consider.

HOW PERSONAL PENSION SCHEMES WORK

As explained in the chapter about non-State pensions, a 'personal' pension is one where there is a contract between the individual and the provider, for a separate pot of money held in your name, without trustees looking after it for you. Personal pensions can be offered by banks, building societies or other financial institutions, but the most usual choice is an insurance company. The employer may help by arranging for a particular provider's contracts to be made available to their employees, and may make a contribution towards them, but is not legally a party to the contract. Personal pensions are always defined-contribution.

Stakeholder pensions are a special type of personal pension. The differences between them and ordinary personal pensions are dealt with on pages 216–220.

You can buy (or have bought for you) a personal pension at any age from birth until your 75th birthday, whether you have any earnings or not, although if you belong to an employer's pension scheme there are special rules about buying a personal pension in addition. You can draw your pension any time between the ages of 50 and 75. This will change to 55 to 75 from 2010, although it will still be possible to draw your pension earlier on the grounds of ill-health.

Until April 2006, HM Revenue & Customs imposes limits on what can go in, rather than on what can come out in pension form. As explained on pages 123–136, however, these limits will change in 2006. Apart from any that may be taken out as a lump sum, the fund that builds up is used to buy an annuity (see pages 237–244), which will provide you with an income for the rest of your life.

The way that personal pensions can be used to contract out of S2P/SERPS was explained on pages 113–114. Before 1988, personal pensions could not be used to contract out of SERPS, and the rules were different. At that time they were called 'Section 226' policies or 'retirement annuities' (see page 216). People who already have these have been allowed to retain them and continue paying in, but no new ones have been started since 1988.

Estimates of your pension

Under the law, you have to be sent a statement each year of how much has gone into your personal pension, and an estimate of how much this will give in retirement. The rules about what has to be shown changed from April 2003 onwards. Annual statements now look different because they take account of how inflation could bite into your pension savings.

In the past, you might have had an estimate, for example, that your pension in 20 years' time, when you retire, will be £10,000 each year. However, if inflation was 2.5 per cent each year between now and then, the £10,000 would only have the buying power of £6,100 at today's prices. This is what the new 'Statutory Money Purchase Illustrations' (SMPIs) show. They are based on a number of assumptions, including:

- your future payments into your pension;
- how your funds might have grown by the time you retire;
- future inflation; and
- how much it could cost to buy a pension income with your pension fund when you retire.

For more information, see *Understanding Your Yearly Pension Statement,* available from the Financial Services Authority (FSA) (see address on page 262).

✳ Action Points

Look for your latest statements, and see how they add up, and what you might expect to get in retirement.

Make some estimates of how much your fund is likely to build up, and how much extra you need to put in to achieve a comfortable retirement, by using one of the 'pension calculators' available on the Internet. Many of the providers include one on their websites, and so do the FSA and the Trades Union Congress (TUC). Look at these to check how your savings are likely to match up with your aspirations, but remember that these are only guesses, based on particular assumptions about inflation and rates of return.

Starting a personal pension

You can pay a lump-sum single premium for a personal pension policy in any year. There is then no further commitment to stick with that provider, and in future years you can shop around for the best arrangement. (At retirement you will usually be able to put the proceeds of all the policies together to buy a single annuity.)

Alternatively, you can sign a contract to pay regular premiums to one pension provider, on a monthly, quarterly or annual basis. This ties you to that contract, and you can find you are penalised if you stop it early.

Tax relief at the basic rate is given directly by HM Revenue & Customs to the pension provider, but the higher-rate element has to be claimed.

When you retire, you can take up to 25 per cent of your pension fund as a tax-free lump sum, and use the rest of the fund to buy yourself an annuity. (This does not change under the new rules explained on pages 123–136.) An annuity is simply a pension paid for life. It may end with your death or, if you have a surviving spouse, carry on until their death. It can remain level or increase each year. The more 'extras' of this sort you add in, the lower the starting amount will be. The different types of annuity you can buy are discussed on pages 237–249.

Types of personal pension policy

There are a number of different types of personal pension policy on the market. Any of these can be 'appropriate' (for contracting out) or non-appropriate.

Deposit-based policies

These are very similar to ordinary savings accounts. Your contributions are saved for you until retirement and earn a variable interest rate for the time when the money is on deposit. There is not usually a penalty for stopping and starting contributions, or for beginning to draw the pension earlier than you originally envisaged. Over the longer term, the returns may be lower than for other forms of policy, but there will not be the same fluctuations as for policies where the money is invested in the stock market.

With-profits policies

The traditional type of insurance policy is the 'with-profits' one where bonuses are added during the lifetime of the policy and cannot then be taken away.

There may also be a final 'terminal' bonus when you draw your pension, although this is not guaranteed and they have been shrinking or disappearing altogether in recent years.

With some older with-profits policies, an underlying guaranteed rate of return was written into the contract at the time you took it out. These guarantees were seen as a sales device, and the insurance companies do not seem to have expected that they would ever come into force. Faced with extra costs, therefore, some insurance companies said that you would only receive the benefit of a guarantee if the terminal bonus were reduced as an offset. This policy was challenged in the courts in the case of Equitable Life, with disastrous results for the company when it lost. There are still question marks over the way some other insurance companies are administering their guarantees.

If you have an existing with-profits policy, look at the small print of the contract to see if you are covered by a guarantee. If so, think carefully about giving up or altering the policy (and take advice), as you are unlikely to be able to replace the guarantee with anything better.

Unitised with-profits policies link the value of the policy to units in a fund. Generally, annual bonuses are also provided, which cannot be taken away once granted. There is, however, at least one 'with-profits' policy on sale where the policy rules do allow for the value to be reduced as well as increased, and some insurers call their products 'with-profits' when there is no smoothing at all, so check the small print.

Unit-linked policies

With this type, your contributions are invested in unit trusts or unit-linked insurance policies, after a deduction for commission and expenses. With unit trusts your money is paid into a pool, from which investment managers buy a range of stocks and shares. Your pension fund at any time will depend on the value of the units at that time. It can therefore go down in value as well as up.

Which type of policy to choose?

In almost everything to do with investment, there is a trade-off between risk and return. If you have certainty or near-certainty of returns, the actual rate of return you get will be low. If you are taking bigger risks, you may get a higher return – or you may get much less. (Think of the way betting on a horse race works.)

For more information on the structure of different sources of investment and of the considerations to take into account, see the Age Concern publication *Your Taxes and Savings* (details on page 269).

Deposit-based and with-profits policies can give a more predictable return than unit-linked policies, but in both cases much depends on the investment performance of the pension fund. Tables of past returns appear in such publications as *Money Management, MoneyFacts* and *Money Marketing*, and current annuity rates are given in *Pensions World* and elsewhere. Future returns can only be an estimate. Research for the Financial Services Authority suggests that the past is a very poor guide to the future, so far as picking 'winners' is concerned – but those who have produced the poorest returns do have a strong chance of continuing to do so.

Unit-linked and with-profits policies are meant for the longer haul; of the two, unit-linked policies are less predictable, while with-profits policies are more stable. Deposit-based policies make safe havens for people nearing retirement who want to consolidate or preserve the pension that has already built up for them, perhaps in a unit-linked fund.

Switching investments

The standard advice for people approaching retirement is to consolidate past investment gains. This means gradually switching your pension fund out of share-based investments into less volatile investments like bonds or gilts.

Most unit-linked personal pensions have a wide range of investment options offering different degrees of investment risk. Some will automatically switch you out of high-risk investments during the last few years before retirement in what is often called a 'lifestyle' arrangement. It is now mandatory for stakeholder schemes to include a 'lifestyle' option. If your policy does not have an automatic switching facility, ask the adviser who sold you the policy for advice on how and when to switch. There may be a charge for switching, but many policies allow you at least one free switch each year.

✳ Action Points

When choosing a personal pension policy:

- look at *Your Taxes and Savings*, and the information on the FSA website, and decide what sort of investments will suit you best (for example, in terms of the risk you are willing to take on); and
- consult an independent financial adviser if you are unsure.

At regular intervals:

- review your investment package and decide whether it still suits you; and
- switch the investments as needed.

Protection for dependants

In an appropriate personal pension scheme, the Protected Rights benefits must include a pension for the widow or widower in the event of the member's death, but this will often be very small. It is also usual to pay over the balance of the fund that has built up from the member's contributions, with or without interest. With any type of personal pension, you need to pay extra premiums if you want to provide life assurance for dependants in the form of a lump sum or a larger continuing pension.

Until April 2006, tax relief is allowed on life assurance premiums of up to 10 per cent of the premium including the life assurance premium itself, within the limits for total contributions to a personal pension scheme. However, under the new 'tax simplification' rules explained on pages 123–136, this relief will no longer exist.

Ill-health

You may be able to draw your pension early on grounds of ill-health, but some providers penalise you heavily for this. With many personal pensions set up before 6 April 2001, a 'waiver of premium benefit' is allowed if you become ill or disabled before 60 or 65. This means that your contributions continue to be paid for as long as you are not earning because of ill-health.

The rules on this changed in April 2001. For policies taken out after that date, a waiver of premium benefit cannot be included in the policy, but you can buy separate insurance to carry on the contributions in both sickness and unemployment. Tax relief will be given when those contributions are paid into the personal pension. Few of these policies are being sold, however, and it may be better value to buy a general 'income protection' policy which gives you control over what you spend the income from the insurance company on, rather than one where the income can only be spent on pension contributions.

You may be able to obtain State benefits if you become unable to work because of disability or sickness, as explained on pages 83–86.

Charges

It is important to look at the charges when taking out a personal pension policy. These cover the provider's costs in setting up the scheme, commission and other payments to those selling you the scheme, and the provider's profits.

As with all consumer purchases, you must shop around and do your research to get the best value for money. The wrong choice will cost you thousands of pounds.

The Financial Services Authority's website (www.fsa.gov.uk) includes a set of comparative tables so that you can see the effect that different insurance companies' charges will have on your final pension.

Regular premiums or single premiums?

You can sign a contract to pay regular premiums into a personal pension scheme over a number of years, or you can pay separate single premiums each year, either to the same provider or to different ones, as you wish. Unless you feel you need the discipline of the contract, it usually makes more sense to pay single premiums. This results in lower initial charges, and also gives you the freedom to switch providers. It could mean that you end up with a whole sheaf of individual policies, but when you draw your pension you will have the option of putting them together into one or buying a number of different annuities.

'Group' personal pensions

'Group' personal pensions (GPPs) are sold by insurance companies to employers who do not want to go to the trouble of setting up a company pension scheme. At their most basic, all they mean is that the employer makes an arrangement with a particular adviser or insurance company so that they sell individual personal pensions to employees during work-time. The employer may 'facilitate' by offering to deduct contributions from your pay at source if you sign up for that package. Sometimes the charges to the individual are no lower than if you bought the policy yourself, but sensible employers will negotiate a better deal to reflect the fact that they are doing much of the work.

The better GPPs also include a substantial extra contribution from the employer, and automatic provision of a lump-sum death benefit and insurance against ill-health.

The rules for stakeholder pensions (explained on pages 216–220) say that if employers already have a GPP for all their staff to which they contribute at least 3 per cent of pay, and where there are no penalties for leaving, they need not offer stakeholder pensions to their employees. This can be conditional on the employee also paying a contribution – this cannot be higher then the employer's own contribution or, for arrangements started since October 2001, the employee cannot be asked to pay more than 3 per cent as a condition for the employer also to contribute.

If you are offered a GPP to which the employer is making a contribution, matching your own or better, it is probably good advice to take it up. The FSA recognises this by allowing a shorter process for signing people up for these pensions. It is still worth checking the details of the policy, however. If the employer is putting in less than this, or if you already have a personal pension which you would be penalised for giving up, it is important that you take independent advice. One possibility would be to contribute a percentage to each policy, rather than putting all your contributions into just one. There are penalties on employers for not paying the members' and their own contributions across quickly, as there are for occupational pensions (see page 198).

✳ Action Points

If you are offered a GPP with your employer:

- find out what the employer contribution is – the more the employer is putting in, the harder you should think before rejecting it;
- look at the investment options available, and the charges, just as you would if you were arranging the policy for yourself; and
- look particularly at what happens to the policy when you leave the employer – will the charges increase?

Self-invested personal pensions (SIPPs)

SIPPs are personal pensions where the policyholders own the investments, rather than the provider doing so and you owning a policy with them. You build up a portfolio of investments out of which your pension will be provided, rather than leaving the pension provider to make the investments. SIPPs are for the richer and more sophisticated investors who can afford the relatively high setting-up costs. One provider quotes typical charges of £600 to set up a SIPP, with an annual administrative fee of £560. There are likely to be investment costs on top of this.

It is possible to convert an ordinary personal pension into a SIPP, and this is being suggested by many advisers because of the changes in the tax rules being made in April 2006. In particular, they are focusing on the fact that, while they have always been allowed to invest in commercial property like offices, shops and industrial units, they will now also be allowed to invest in residential property.

However, it is important to realise that:

- the fund must have the money in it already in order to do so (although it can borrow up to 50 per cent of the value of the fund, so a fund with £200,000 in it could borrow £100,000 and buy a property for £300,000);
- a market rent must be paid to the fund for any period of time when the member or the member's family is using it; and
- eventually, the property will need to be sold to provide an income for the member, either by buying an annuity or by creating a flow of alternatively secured pension (see page 245). The latest you can delay drawing income from a SIPP is at age 75.

One example being quoted is that someone could buy a holiday property, in the UK or overseas, let it commercially for most of the year but use it themselves for a few weeks each year. This would be allowed, *provided that* the SIPP holder paid the market rent for the times when he or she was using the property. The SIPP could also buy a property for the member's children to use whilst at university, again so long as a market rent was paid.

Some advisers are suggesting that people should even put their *owner-occupied* homes into a SIPP. This seems unlikely to be wise, however, as it would mean:

- paying market rent to your pension fund; and
- selling it on the market when you reach 75 at the latest, regardless of whether a move suited you at this time.

The investment and administrative functions of SIPPs are separated (whereas in other personal pensions you buy a package deal). You can therefore switch investment managers as well as or instead of the actual investments. This can be very important for people in professional partnerships and similar managerial positions. The usual range of investments is available. Take professional advice before setting one up.

✳ Action Points

If you are thinking of setting up a SIPP, and especially if you are thinking of including residential property in it:

- take specialist advice, from those with no axe to grind rather than from people who want to sell you the idea;
- be especially careful if dealing with property abroad, where the tax rules could negate the tax advantages in the UK; and
- think very carefully about the 'exit route'; in other words, when you would want to start drawing an income from the fund and how you would go about it.

Section 226 policies

Before 1988, self-employed people and those not in an employer's scheme were able to take out personal pension policies known as Section 226 retirement annuity policies. These are no longer available, but if you have one or more you are allowed to keep them going.

Until April 2006, you may be able to draw a larger lump sum from a Section 226 policy than the 25 per cent maximum allowed with a personal pension. On the other hand, Section 226 policies do not allow you to draw a pension before the age of 60, whereas with personal pensions the earliest age is 50 (55 from 2010 onwards).

You can transfer a Section 226 policy into a personal pension if the insurer's rules allow this, but it means sacrificing part of the lump sum. You may also be able to alter your policy if its original terms no longer suit you – for example to provide larger death benefits and a smaller pension. This will depend on the terms of your policy. Make sure you get advice before doing this.

STAKEHOLDER PENSIONS

Stakeholder pensions are a special sort of personal pension, which the Government has targeted at those earning between about £12,100 and £27,800 who are not in an occupational pension scheme. They began in April 2001, with two important features:

- legal requirements on employers to give people access to a scheme through the workplace, and to make deductions from pay and pass them on; and
- strict government regulation on what can be charged.

However, employers are *not* required to contribute to stakeholder schemes.

The main details of stakeholder pensions are:

- A percentage of each individual's fund is deducted by those running the scheme, to cover all normal operating costs. For policies that have already been taken out, the maximum is 1 per cent a year, and in fact many stakeholder arrangements charge rather less, at least for larger funds. However, for new policies taken out after April 2005, the maximum has risen to 1.5 per cent for the first 10 years of a policy, after which it drops back to 1 per cent. (This is because the providers convinced the Government that they were not making sufficient profits on stakeholder pensions to be able to sell them actively.)
- The minimum contribution level must be no higher than £20, and there must be no minimum frequency of contributions.
- There must be no charges or penalties for transfers, and stakeholder schemes must accept transfers from other schemes. However, since April 2005 'with-profits' stakeholder schemes have been allowed to make a 'market value adjustment' (MVA) – in other words, to reduce the pot of money you can take if you want to transfer your money elsewhere, or if you retire early.

Stakeholder pensions can offer a range of investment options, but they must include one or more 'default funds', into which anyone who does not want to make an active choice is automatically enrolled. The default funds must include a 'lifestyle' arrangement (see pages 98–99). Default funds vary considerably between providers, and some are invested in a more risky package of investments than would generally be recommended, certainly for older investors. Lifestyle arrangements are similarly a 'one size fits all' arrangement and do not suit everyone. They can, for example, require you to choose your retirement age at the start of the policy, with little or no opportunity for changing your mind. However, around 80 per cent of all purchasers take up the 'default' options without making any further choices.

✳ Action Points

Check out what the investment packages are, and select the ones that suit you, rather than simply going with the default fund.

Look closely at the lifestyle arrangement; if it does not give enough flexibility for you, do not take it up. You can tailor-make your own 'lifestyle' arrangement by gradually shifting your investments between funds as you get older.

Access via the employer

If an employer has five or more employees, it must provide a stakeholder scheme, within three months of starting work, if there is not an occupational scheme that employees are entitled to join after a waiting period of up to a year. The occupational scheme is also allowed to exclude those aged under 18 or within five years of starting retirement.

Group Personal Pensions (GPPs) can also exempt the employer from providing access to a stakeholder scheme, provided that the employer is contractually committed to make a contribution of 3 per cent or more of basic pay and that the individual will not be penalised for stopping payments into the scheme. The employer can require the individual to make a contribution to the GPP as well, but cannot insist that this is more than 3 per cent of basic pay. However, if the scheme was set up before 8 October 2001 (the start date for these rules), the employer can make it a condition that the employee contributes at a higher level than this, but not at a higher rate than the employer does. So, for example, a scheme which already existed before October 2001 could have an employer contribution of 8 per cent and an employee contribution of 4 per cent, and still provide exemption for the employer.

'Access' means that the employer 'designates' a scheme. You can then ask the employer to make a deduction from your pay, and pass the money over to that designated scheme within a time limit. If an employer changes the designated scheme, it must continue to pass on contributions to the old one if the employees want it to. An employer is not required, however, to pass on contributions to any other scheme, so if you want to deal with a different provider, you will need to make some other arrangement, such as a direct debit.

Where the employer is making the deductions, individuals will only be able to change their contribution levels every six months at most, although they can always insist that their contributions are stopped immediately.

Stakeholder schemes are regulated by the Pensions Regulator (tPR), as with occupational schemes. The people selling them have to follow rules laid down by the Financial Services Authority (see page 223), as with personal pensions. There are some special rules (under the *Financial Promotions Order 2005*), for employers communicating with their employees about GPPs and stakeholder schemes. Employers are exempt from the usual tight FSA rules about promoting financial products, provided that they:

- are making a contribution to the employees' pension policies, and have told them how much it will be; and
- are not receiving any financial benefit from the scheme (such as a share of any commission paid by the insurance company).

(This does not mean, of course, that they can make statements they know to be untrue.)

A few stakeholder pension schemes, including the one being run by the TUC particularly for trade union members, are 'trust based', and the rules say that one-third of their trustees must be independent (see pages 104–105 for an explanation of what trustees do). Most schemes, however, are contract-based, and run by large insurance companies or other commercial providers.

Finding out more about stakeholder pensions

The DWP has a leaflet called *A Guide to Your Pension Options* (PM1), and another one called *Stakeholder Pensions: Your Guide* (PM8). You can order these by phoning 0845 731 3233.

The FSA has a factsheet called *Stakeholder Pensions and Decision Trees*, which you can use to go through the question of whether a stakeholder pension is right for you. The FSA's consumer helpline is on 0845 606 1234.

The Pensions Advisory Service (TPAS) also has a helpline on 0845 601 2923. Calls are charged at local rates, and the line is open between 9.00am–5.00pm, Monday to Friday. However, the helpline cannot provide specific financial advice.

The Pensions Regulator (tPR) has a website (www.thepensionsregulator.gov.uk/stakeholderpensions) which has information and links leading you through to other official sites and also to the register of all the different providers and to the providers' own websites.

BUYING A PERSONAL PENSION

Since personal pensions are complex and you do not see the results of your purchase for several decades, it is generally wise to get some financial advice before signing up for one.

Advice on stakeholder pensions

For the more straightforward 'stakeholder' pension, it is assumed that in many cases detailed advice will not be necessary. It is not covered by the normal charges for a stakeholder pension, so if you want such advice you may need to pay extra.

Decision trees

To help people decide whether a stakeholder pension would be a good choice for them, there are consumer factsheets containing 'decision trees' for employed people, the self-employed and people who are not employed but who might be able to contribute to a personal pension, available on the FSA's website at www.fsa.gov.uk

The decision trees are in two parts. The introductory notes explain what a stakeholder pension is and how it works. The notes also give details of the State Pension scheme and list some of the questions that you might want to ask. The actual decision trees follow, and include questions about your pension arrangements and circumstances. Answering these will help you think about your pension options. The decision trees give some pension estimates based on your age and how much you can afford to contribute regularly to a stakeholder pension.

If you simply fill in a form for a personal pension or stakeholder pension and send it with a cheque, no extra advice or information will be offered by the provider, although the cost to you will be the same as if you bought as part of an 'advised' sale. So before doing this, read the FSA's factsheet, or take yourself through a decision tree. If you make an enquiry to a provider or an independent financial adviser about taking out a stakeholder pension, the firms selling them will be required by the FSA to make sure that customers have decision trees in front of them when being taken through the process over the telephone. The outcome will have to be confirmed in writing, with a copy of the route taken through the tree included. Where an adviser recommends a traditional personal pension, perhaps a Group Personal Pension, currently the adviser must include in the letter an explanation of why this was considered at least as good an option as a stakeholder pension. The FSA, however, is proposing to abolish this requirement, despite acknowledging the risk that charges may rise as a result.

Getting good financial advice

It is a good idea to take advice when buying a personal pension or an annuity, but how do you ensure that you are getting good advice?

'Fact-finds' (questionnaires about your financial circumstances) are a legal requirement, but they are also useful to advisers as a marketing exercise, because they can gather information on what other products they might be able to sell to you. Treat your advisers with caution, and don't be afraid to question them closely and to say that you will go away and think about things.

Advisers who are doing their job properly will complete a detailed fact-find. This should include details about your whole financial position, and especially about whether you have an employer's pension scheme open to you. If they do not do this, or if they play it down as 'just a formality', treat them with extreme caution. However, where the employer is making a contribution to a Group Personal Pension, the FSA does allow a 'fast track' procedure without the full fact-find.

How financial advisers are paid

Most financial advisers work on commission, which means that part of your payment goes to them without ever going to the insurance company or other provider.

Independent financial advisers currently have three main sources of commission income:

1. **'Initial commission'**, which in practice is around 3 per cent.
2. **'Renewal commission'**, which is a commission paid on regular premiums, typically in the range of 1.5 per cent to 2.5 per cent.
3. **'Trail commission'**, payable in theory for an ongoing advice role and which is paid on the total fund value, typically in the range of 0.5 per cent to 1.5 per cent per year.

For stakeholder pensions, whatever commission the insurance company pays to the adviser, the cost to you can be no more than 1.5 per cent of the fund per year for the first 10 years, and 1 per cent after that.

It is also increasingly common to pay your financial adviser an up-front fee instead, and have the amount you would otherwise have paid in commission added back to your premiums or paid to you in cash. The fee could be £200 or more, but it may well be worth it to get unbiased advice. Many advisers will offer the first half-hour free.

Recent rule changes

There are a number of legal rules about the way that financial advice can be given, and the information that must be provided, laid down by the Financial Services Authority. These rules changed considerably, however, in December 2004. The restrictions have been removed on the advice service firms can offer and on the information that firms have to give to consumers about their financial advice services.

Previously, advisers could only offer 'independent' or 'tied' advice. Independent advisers offered advice on products from the whole of the market, whereas 'tied' advisers were limited to the products of only one provider. Since 1 December 2004 it has been possible for firms to offer advice:

- covering the whole of the market;
- from a limited number of providers; or
- from a single provider.

At the beginning of the sales process, you must be given information that will help you to understand what service you are being offered; give you an indication of what you will have to pay for it; and help you to compare prices and shop around for the best value.

This information will be included in two '**key**facts' documents. The first, called '**key**facts about our services', will explain the advice service your adviser is offering, and the range of products they offer advice on.

The second, '**key**facts about the cost of our services', will tell you:

- the different ways of paying for advice;
- an indication of the fees or commission you may have to pay; and
- if you pay by commission, show how the commission cost compares to the market average commission.

Advisers who want to continue to describe themselves as 'independent' must be able to advise on products from across the whole market and they must offer you the opportunity to pay by fee instead of commission.

The rules cover advice on certain investment products (called 'packaged products'), which include life assurance, personal and stakeholder pensions, endowments, collective investment schemes, and ISAs (where life assurance and collective investment schemes are components).

It is up to each firm whether they want to change their advice service. It seems likely that high street firms currently giving advice from one product provider will expand their product range, and that most 'independent' advisers will stay as they are. The new rules were implemented over a six-month transitional period, beginning on 1 December 2004. During this time firms could either choose to change or not. However, from 1 June 2005, all firms have to offer the '**key**facts' documents.

For more information, see the *FSA Guide to Financial Advice,* which is available free from the FSA at the address on page 262 or on its website. The FSA has a central register that details what kind of business a financial adviser is authorised to do. You can call the FSA consumer helpline to check that any particular adviser is properly authorised. The Institute of Financial Planning (address on page 266) runs a national register of fee-based financial planners.

Duties of independent financial advisers

Independent financial advisers are legally supposed to stick to three principles:

Best advice They should find out enough about your personal circumstances to enable them to give advice about what is best for you, regardless of whether it brings them a high level of commission or not.

Best execution Where a product is available at more than one price, they should shop around, find the best bargain, and pass on the savings to you.

Suitability The product must be suitable for your needs.

You normally have a 'cooling off' period in which you can cancel the deal without penalty. You must be told clearly what this period is.

If you are not satisfied that an independent adviser is fulfilling these duties, you can complain first to the compliance officer within their firm and then to the Financial Ombudsman Service (address on page 262).

How to make sure you get the best advice

You will get the best service from a financial adviser if you already know what you are looking for. Think about whether you should sign a regular premium contract or pay single premiums each year. Ask about:

- charging structure;
- taking earlier or later retirement;

- increasing or decreasing your premiums; and
- what benefit is payable on death.

When you have chosen a product, you should be given a buyer's guide giving all its details. Dull as it is likely to be, it will be worth checking through it and questioning anything on which you are not clear.

If you are offered an appropriate personal pension (to contract out of S2P) or if you are being pressed to transfer from your employer's scheme, ask for a specific written statement about why the adviser is recommending this.

Normally, you would make any payment cheque out to the insurance company or other provider, not to the financial adviser. Be very cautious if the adviser suggests you pay them.

Compensation for mis-selling

If you have not been given 'best advice' and as a result you have suffered a financial loss, you may be able to obtain compensation from the firm responsible. This has happened, for example, in cases where people have been wrongly transferred out of their employer's pension scheme. It will usually take the form of a payment back to the employer's scheme in return for accepting you back into membership, or as a top-up to a personal pension, rather than cash in hand. There is a system of levies on advisers and financial institutions to cover compensation where firms have gone out of existence.

Complaints about personal and stakeholder pensions

The Pensions Ombudsman deals with complaints about maladministration in personal pensions (see address on page 264).

The Financial Ombudsman Service (FOS) deals with individual complaints about the sales and marketing of these products. The FOS can help consumers resolve complaints about most personal finance matters. The service is independent, flexible, informal and free for consumers – the address is on page 262.

Stamping out bad or illegal sales practices by providers is the responsibility of the FSA.

If you are not sure who you should go to, phone TPAS at the number on page 264, and it will redirect you.

Consumer publications from the Financial Services Authority

The FSA has a range of guides and factsheets aimed at consumers. These give simple explanations and the information you need to ask the right questions and make informed choices when buying financial products and services. You can order them by phoning the FSA, or if you have access to the Internet, you can also download them from the FSA website at the address on page 262.

People with broken employment records

You may feel, like many others today, that you have little job security and are likely to go through a series of short-term jobs, periods of self-employment and periods of unemployment during what remains of your working life. If so, it will be doubly important to choose the right sort of personal pension or stakeholder pension policy in order to maximise your income during retirement.

When you take out a pension, you can either sign a contract with the insurance company (or other pension provider) to pay regular premiums over a period of years or you can pay a single premium in one lump sum each year, with no commitment to go back to the same provider in following years. If your employment prospects are uncertain, it will make better sense to buy a single-premium policy each year. If you find the idea of making a large pension payment all at once too daunting, open a building society account and start a standing order to make regular payments to it each month. Then you can pay the whole lot into a pension policy at the end of the year. If you want to make regular premiums, then you will want a policy that does not penalise you for starting and stopping. This would generally mean a stakeholder pension (explained on pages 216–220).

You can make contributions to a personal pension scheme even during tax years in which you have no 'net relevant earnings'. With non-stakeholder personal pensions, some regular-premium policies impose penalties if there are gaps in contributions, and may even require you to make the policy 'paid up' (see page 233). Alternatively, use single-premium policies and put in as much as you can afford (within the annual allowance explained on page 122) in later years to make up for earlier gaps.

Even if you see no prospect of a career with one employer, you may well have periods of work with employers that have pension schemes, and it would be unfortunate if you had to pass up the opportunity to join (and get the benefit of the employer's contribution) because you were paying into a personal pension.

You could either take out a single-premium personal pension each year when you do not have an employer's pension available to you, or ensure that you have a personal or stakeholder pension policy that makes no charges for starting and stopping contributions.

✳ Action Points

If you are planning to buy a personal pension:

- work out what you need, which of the various options will suit you best, and how much you can sensibly afford to pay as a contribution;
- put together also a note of your other financial commitments and investments, so you can see the whole picture;
- decide how you want to pay for your financial advice (commission or fee), and whether you want to be offered a restricted range of products or ones from the whole of the market;
- make appointments with two or three advisers who seem suitable, for a preliminary discussion;
- having established which one suits you best, arrange an in-depth discussion; and
- if they ask you to make your pension contribution cheque out to them rather than the provider, or if they give what is clearly unsuitable advice in your circumstances, complain to the Financial Services Authority.

ISSUES FOR WOMEN

Personal pension contributions

Women's career patterns are often disrupted by caring for children and other dependants. You are allowed to pay into a personal pension (including a stakeholder scheme) even if you are not earning, as explained on page 122. However, even with the best of intentions you may find that the family finances are under too much of a strain to allow this. So if you take out a personal or stakeholder pension policy, you need to ensure that it is one that does not charge extra for the first few years, or penalise you for stopping payments. It may be better to make contributions through a series of single premiums rather than committing yourself to regular premiums.

If you were already paying into a personal pension scheme before the tax rules changed, and want to start a family, or have to take time away from work for other reasons, check what happens if there is a gap in your contributions. Some personal pension providers penalise you heavily.

You may find that waiver of premium benefit (see page 211) does not apply in cases of maternity or pregnancy-related illnesses. Although this is discriminatory, it is not unlawful under European law, because your personal pension is not an employment-related benefit. (But if the employer is contributing towards it, this is a grey area in the law where there might be a challenge sooner or later in the European Court of Justice.)

Contracting out of S2P

As explained on page 119, women need to be very cautious about taking out an appropriate personal pension to contract out of S2P. Their longer life expectancy and lower average earnings mean that in general staying with S2P is the better policy.

Pensions and divorce

Personal and stakeholder pensions can be divided under the 'pension-sharing' rules explained on pages 158–160. For these, it will mean dividing the money in the fund so that each partner can have their own 'pot' and build up a pension on their own account.

✳ Action Points

Before you start with a personal or stakeholder pension:

- check the position if you were to stop paying into the policy for several years;
- arrange either to take out a policy which will not penalise you for this, or to pay single premiums each year, without signing a regular premium contract; and
- consider whether to contract out of S2P or not, but be cautious before doing so, especially if your earnings are low.

When you stop working, consider whether you can continue to carry on paying contributions into your personal pension (or if your husband/partner can do this for you).

WORKING AFTER RETIREMENT AGE

Most personal or stakeholder pensions will include a specified retirement age as part of the policy. If you are still working at that age, you may want to defer drawing the personal pension and possibly also continue to contribute towards it. However, it is important to check if this is the best thing to do. There are penalties on deferring in some older-style personal pensions, and you may not gain enough in improved annuity rates to make up for the lack of payments for several years. An alternative would be to start drawing it but to put the income into other forms of savings (or even another pension) until you need it.

It is possible to continue paying into a personal pension until you reach the age of 75. Until April 2006, you can put in up to 40 per cent of your earnings and receive tax relief. After that date, the contribution limits increase, as explained on pages 123–136. When you come to draw the pension you will be able to collect a tax-free lump sum as well as an income, so it can be very tax-effective.

However, as the money will only be in the fund for a fairly short time, you need to ensure that the pension contract you sign is suitable, and does not penalise short-stayers.

The rules on 'income drawdown', explained on pages 245–246, could be useful for someone who wants to take partial retirement. Another way of achieving the same end is to buy 'clusters' of personal pension policies. A number of insurance companies will arrange their contracts in this way. You then start to draw on as many as suits you at any one time.

✱ Action Points

If you continue working beyond the age at which you can draw your personal pension:

- get advice on whether deferring it is worthwhile;
- decide on whether to continue paying into that, or into another personal pension policy; and
- consider the possibilities of income drawdown or buying a 'cluster' of pension policies to finance a partial retirement.

STOPPING PAYING INTO A PERSONAL PENSION

If you start work for a new employer who has an occupational pension scheme, it will usually be best to join it where possible, as explained on pages 146–148.

Until April 2006, there are some restrictions on belonging to an occupational and a personal scheme at the same time. It is possible to join an occupational scheme and put up to £3,600 into a personal pension as well, provided you have earned under £30,000 a year in one of the previous five years, with 2000–2001 being the first year to count, and are not a controlling director of the company. After that date, you will be able to pay as much as you want, to as many different pension arrangements as you want, so long as you do not go above the limits explained on pages 123–136. The chief considerations for most people now, therefore, are what they can afford, and whether there are any penalties on stopping or transferring the personal pension.

For a stakeholder pension (explained on pages 216–220) there can be no penalties for starting and stopping payments, but for some non-stakeholder personal pensions there may be a penalty for stopping the contract early. If your personal pension policy has not been running for long, you may find that very little has gone into your fund yet in any case, as your payments have been eaten up by commission and charges. There may also be a continuing annual administration charge, which can eat away quite badly at a paid-up pension.

The options if you have a personal pension and do not want to continue paying into it at the same time as belonging to the employer's scheme, are to:

- suspend the contributions and restart them at some future date (there may be a time limit on this);
- make the policy 'paid up', which means that the provider's charges and commission are deducted from your fund, and the rest is left to accrue investment returns until you are able to draw the pension and lump sum; or
- transfer the money from the personal pension policy into your new employer's scheme (if the scheme will accept it).

Of all the options, suspending contributions may be the least financially damaging. Doing this rather than making the policy paid up, if your contract allows you to do so, may result in lower deductions.

When you take out a personal pension policy, you have by law to be given a Buyer's Guide which gives projected figures for what will be in the fund over the next few years if you want to transfer it, including columns showing the amounts that will be deducted. The actual figures may be different if the investment results are different (either better or worse). Look back at this to see what the costs of a transfer would be.

If your policy has been running for a number of years and you have built up a substantial fund, the choice can be more difficult. You may need to negotiate with the pension provider and the new employer (possibly with the help of an actuary) to find the best deal.

None of these considerations applies if you have been paying a series of single premiums without a commitment to making regular payments. In that case, your fund will simply continue to be invested, with whatever charges are included.

Stopping work

You may become unemployed or want to take early retirement. The current contribution limits (which end on the last day of the 2005–2006 tax year) apply for each tax year, so if you lose your job part of the way through the tax year, you can use the earnings in that year as a figure on which to calculate your pension contribution. It could be worth using part of any redundancy payment or similar lump sum for this purpose.

You can continue paying contributions even if you are not earning – although this change in the tax rules does not solve the problem of whether you will be able to afford them.

If you have bought waiver of premium benefit (explained on page 211), this should safeguard you against being penalised for a gap in contributions if you are committed to paying regular premiums. Otherwise, investigate the alternatives of suspending contributions or making the policy paid up (see page 233) if yours is a non-stakeholder personal pension that may penalise you for either.

If you are 50 or over (55 from 2010 onwards), you will usually have the option of starting to draw the pension and lump sum from the policy. There will usually be a substantial reduction, however, if this is being paid early, so it may be better to wait if you can afford to. Check the terms of your policy.

✳ Action Points

If you start work for a new employer with a pension scheme you can join:

- consider whether you can afford to carry on paying into the personal pension at the same time as joining the occupational scheme;
- look at the policy documents, or ask your financial adviser or insurance company, what penalties there would be on stopping, suspending or changing your contributions, or making the policy paid up;
- find out from your employer's pensions department whether they are willing to take in a transfer value, and how much pension you would get in exchange; and
- decide what to do, with the help of an actuary if you need to negotiate.

If you are going to stop work:

- consider using part of any redundancy or severance payment to add to your personal pension;
- find out if you have waiver of premium benefit. If not, consider the other alternatives (see above); and
- if you are old enough, look at the option of starting to draw your pension and lump sum, and how big the actuarial reductions would be.

INCREASING YOUR PENSION

Personal pensions have generous contribution limits, which will be more generous from April 2006.

Employees may be able to persuade their employer to make a contribution, although not many do so. There can be tax advantages for both employer and employee in doing this. Employer contributions to a retirement benefit scheme (including a personal pension) are not taxable as income to the employee. Nor are NI contributions payable on the amount of the employer's contributions. The employer will also be able to obtain tax relief on contributions as a business expense.

It is possible to carry on paying into a personal pension even if you are not earning, with a contribution of up to £3,600 a year.

✳ Action Points

If your income goes up, or your financial commitments go down, consider whether you can increase your regular contributions to your personal or stakeholder pension.

If you have a windfall such as an inheritance, think about using some or all of it for a one-off payment into a personal pension (but check your tax position; if it is a large amount, you may need to spread it over two or more tax years).

DRAWING YOUR PENSION

When you draw a personal pension, certain choices are open to you. You can choose whether to take the maximum permitted lump sum and you can also choose which type of annuity to buy and which company to buy it from. This gives you a range of options in respect of retirement benefits.

The lump sum

With a personal pension, the maximum part of your pension fund that may be taken as a tax-free lump sum is usually 25 per cent. Until April 2006, the Protected Rights element in an appropriate personal pension (APP – see page 113) must be used to buy a pension, and with one of the older Section 226 policies it could be more than the usual maximum. Unless there is a huge disparity in the annuity rates offered, people usually stay with the policy that gives the larger lump sum, because of the tax advantage.

Buying an annuity

The rest of the money built up in a personal pension fund must be used to provide your retirement income. For most people, this means buying an annuity. It is also possible to use your tax-free lump sum (or other capital) to purchase an additional annuity. This can have tax advantages, as part of the payment is treated as a return of your own capital and is therefore tax free.

For some people, it could be worth giving the tax-free lump sum to their spouse or partner to buy an annuity with, especially if the two of you are in different tax brackets. There would be a number of considerations to take into account in doing this, however, so you would need to take independent financial advice.

By law, only insurance companies, and not other personal pension providers, can provide annuities. Annuity rates vary with age. The younger you are when you purchase an annuity, the less income you will get; the older you are, the bigger the income. Annuity rates for women are lower than for men (except for the Protected Rights element, where rates must be equal) because women's longer average life expectancy means that they are likely to be paid the income for longer. This practice is allowed under the *Sex Discrimination Act*.

You do not have to buy your annuity from the pension provider to whom you have paid your pension contributions. You will have an 'open market option' (OMO) which allows you to choose any insurance company where the annuity rates may be better. Your original pension provider normally provides the tax-free lump sum, and the rest of your pension fund is then transferred at retirement under a 'substitution contract' to provide your pension. All providers have to inform consumers of their right to shop around for the best annuity rate (the OMO) well in advance of their retirement date. Insurance companies should also explain the different types of annuity available, under their own code of good practice. The FSA publishes comparative tables of annuity rates (www.fsa.gov.uk/tables), which make it easier for consumers to shop around.

Which type of annuity?

The right choice of annuity can affect your retirement income considerably, as well as your peace of mind. An independent financial adviser (one who looks across the whole market and is not linked to any specific providers) should be able to 'shop around' for you and find the best value available at the time (see pages 222–226). However, you will get better advice if you have worked out your requirements already.

There are a number of different types of annuities, and several new types have come on the market in the last few years. The new tax reforms (explained on pages 123–136) should also mean that more flexible annuities become available.

Annuities that are not linked to investment return

Once you have bought an annuity not linked to the returns on the capital invested, the terms are fixed. There are choices to be made before you buy:

- Do you want a high starting level that remains fixed for the rest of your life or a lower one that increases by a percentage each year? (If you want a pension linked to the Retail Prices Index, the starting level will be lower still.)

Retirement income products

Non-investment linked annuities

Flat annuity	Provides a fixed level of income for life, but does not increase over time.
Escalating annuity	Fixed annual rises at, for example, 3% or 5%, without investment risk.
RPI-linked annuity	Rises linked to the RPI, without investment risk.
Limited price indexed annuity	A RPI link but capped (often at 5%), without investment risk.
Dependant's benefits	Provides income after the pensioner's death for a spouse or dependent children.
Guaranteed period annuities	Promises to pay the annuity for a predetermined period of up to 10 years, whether the pensioner survives or not.
Smokers' annuities	Provides higher annuities to people who have smoked an average of 10 cigarettes a day for the last 10 years.
Impaired life annuities	Provides higher annuities for people with certain medical conditions limiting their life expectancy.

Investment-linked products

With-profits annuity	Two components – guaranteed minimum and bonuses. Requires the annuitant to choose a quite complex assumed bonus rate (ABR).
Unit-linked annuities with investment choices, eg high, medium or tracker	Generally regarded as high risk, but still with different degrees of risk, depending on investment choices.
Drawdown	Highest risk.

(Source: adapted from *Modernising Annuities: A Consultative Document – Inland Revenue*, February 2002)

- Do you want a guarantee that the pension will be paid for a minimum length of time – perhaps five or ten years?
- Do you want the pension for yourself alone or do you want it to continue until your spouse's death (called a 'joint-life and survivor' pension)?
- Do you want to get a slightly higher rate in return for taking your income 12 months in arrears, or do you prefer to play for safety and get very much less in return for being paid a year in advance?
- Do you want payments monthly or quarterly?
- Do you want an annuity which starts slightly lower, but then increases because you need long-term care?
- (After April 2006) Do you want a 'limited period' annuity – for example to run for five years until some other income source kicks in?
- (After April 2006) Do you want an annuity which starts slightly lower, but will give the remaining capital back should you die before the age of 75?

All these options are possible, and will affect the income you get from your annuity. Other factors such as interest rates and your age, health and sex will also affect it.

It is also possible to get a better rate if you fall into a special category – such as being a lifelong smoker. Since this reduces your life expectancy, there are insurance companies which offer higher annuity rates, perhaps increased by as much as a quarter. Similarly, if you are an 'impaired life' (in the insurance company's terms) for any other reason, such as having a heart condition, you may be able to get a better rate.

The table overleaf shows how the rates vary between men and women, people of different ages, and different types. The rates here are the best rates available in that particular week for 'compulsory purchase' annuities, which are those purchased from your fund at the time you start your pension. There is another sort – 'purchased life' – which you can buy with any other sort of capital, and for which the price and the tax situation (as explained on page 244) are different. The figures below are for the first year's pension, as an annual figure, provided in return for a capital payment of £10,000.

Gender/age	Level annuity, without guarantee	Level annuity, guaranteed for 5 years*	Annuity increasing by 5% a year (no guarantee) – starting rate
Man aged 60	£603.12	£600.72	£325.80
Woman aged 60	£564.24	£562.68	£283.32
Joint life (man aged 60, woman aged 55)	£546.96	£545.04	£266.92

(Source: *The Annuity Bureau – www.annuity-bureau.co.uk – July 2005*)

The guarantee here is that the pension will continue to be paid for a minimum of 5 years, even if the individual dies before that.

Investment-linked annuities

These come in several types, and new varieties are coming onto the market all the time.

Unit-linked annuities

Unit-linked annuities are available from a limited range of insurers. The annual income from this type of annuity depends on the value of the units in the underlying fund, so it can vary considerably. If you are of an optimistic nature, a unit-linked annuity might suit you. In the long term, it could provide an element of growth that is missing from level-rate annuities. But the income fluctuates with the fortunes of the stock market, so you should not expect to be able to rely on it for basic living costs.

With-profits annuities

An even more limited range of companies offer 'with-profits' annuities, sometimes only to existing policyholders. These give a fairly low guaranteed income plus annual bonuses from the with-profits fund. The initial income may be raised by anticipating a higher annual bonus, but if the bonus turns out to be lower than expected your annual income will also be lower, and vice versa for a bonus that proves to be higher than expected.

Other new types of annuity

One insurance company has an annuity that allows you to change the bonus rate (see above) up to three times – perhaps by becoming more cautious as you get older. Another allows you to buy 'temporary' annuities lasting five years at a time, so that the rates and terms can be changed as you get older. A more recently launched product puts most of the money into the financial markets, so that the income can go up or down, and adds a certain amount of money as you get older (called a 'mortality subsidy' and coming from the funds of those who die before you).

Investment-linked annuities carry risks, but they do allow you to share investment gains if the stock market does well. You could see them as a half-way house between a conventional annuity and the riskier income drawdown (covered on pages 245–246). They are complex products, so it is very important that you take advice, and understand fully what you are going into. They account for a small percentage of all the annuities bought.

What happens on your death?

If you buy a 'joint-life' annuity, this continues until the death of both parties. This is the type that married couples should therefore buy. When one of the couple dies, there are a number of variations in what happens next. Check the policy details to be sure you are buying what you want.

With either a single-life or a joint-life policy, you can buy:

- a 'with proportion' annuity, which offers a proportion of the next instalment of the annuity if you die between payments;
- one that guarantees to pay some or all of the payments for a minimum number of years – often either five or ten years – even if you die before this; or
- one that makes a payment of the difference between your original outlay and the income so far paid out by the company – called a 'value-protected' annuity (after April 2006).

Costs of annuities

The rule of thumb is that the standard annuity is a level-rate one, covering only a single person and dying with them. You pay more for any additional features in that you have to accept a lower starting income. So you must weigh up their real value to you.

Tax restrictions on annuities

HM Revenue & Customs imposes some restrictions on the type of annuity you buy:

- If you choose one which gives you an income for a guaranteed period, that period cannot exceed ten years.
- The continuing payments to a surviving spouse or partner must not be larger than the original pension. So, for example, if you buy a

pension of £100 a month, you cannot arrange for the surviving spouse to receive a pension of more than that amount.

- After April 2006, the cost of the annuity must be tested against the Lifetime Allowance explained on pages 123–127.

HM Revenue & Customs also makes a distinction between two main types of annuity:

- **A compulsory purchase annuity** is bought with the proceeds of an employer's pension scheme or a personal pension. The income from this kind of annuity is taxed as earned income.
- **A purchased life annuity** is bought with your own capital at a time to suit yourself – even though you may be using the tax-free lump sum from your pension fund. Part of the income from a purchased life annuity is treated as repayment of capital and therefore untaxed.

The capital element of a purchased life annuity will be read off a table of 'actuarial values' drawn up by HM Revenue & Customs. For each yearly instalment, the capital element is taken to be the amount of the purchase price, divided by the number of years equivalent to the purchaser's life expectancy at the beginning of the annuity.

Example

Brian is aged 70. His purchased life annuity costs £20,000 and provides him with a pension for life of £1,505.88 per year. His age gives the policy an actuarial value of £21,135.16. This is the total amount of income Brian will receive from the annuity if he lives the anticipated number of years. The yearly capital element is £1,505.88 x 20,000/21,135.16 or £1,425. More simply, you could say that HMRC expects him to live another 14 years, so if you divide £20,000 by 14 you arrive at the same result. This part of his annuity income is then free of Income Tax.

Drawing unsecured income

It is possible to take a pension directly out of your fund, without buying an annuity. At present, this can only be done until age 75 and is called 'income drawdown', or sometimes 'income withdrawal'. At the age of 75, you must buy an annuity with what remains of the fund. There are tight minimum and maximum limits on the amount taken out each year, related to the amount you could have had from an annuity, and also a requirement for a regular review at least every three years.

After April 2006, the rules change to say that you must not take out more than 120 per cent of the relevant annuity that could have been bought. A 'relevant annuity' is the highest annual income that could be bought for a non-smoking individual of that age and sex, and must be reviewed every five years.

After April 2006, when someone reaches age 75, they will be able to take an 'alternatively secured pension' (ASP) directly from the fund. The amount cannot exceed more than 70 per cent of the relevant annuity. Any funds left over after death can be used to benefit other family members, but within some tight restrictions. The family members must be members of the same pension scheme, and any distribution to fewer than 200 members within a scheme will incur a 40 per cent tax charge. The leftover funds cannot be received as cash, but must remain in the scheme for use when the beneficiary retires.

Most advisers would say that it is not even worth thinking about income drawdown unless you have a pension fund of more than about £200,000, as the charges for managing the investment, and for advice, will eat too far into a smaller fund. There are some campaigners, however, who would regard annuities generally as poor value and claim that income withdrawal is suitable for people with much lower funds, so long as they have other sources of income as well.

A major difference between an annuity and an unsecured pension is that with an annuity you are buying insurance against living too long, whereas with income drawdown you are on your own. With an annuity, you are putting yourself in a group of people (all the annuity holders with that company), some of whom will live only a few years, some of whom will live for many years. Those who die earlier have their surplus funds redistributed among those who live longer, and the annuity rates are set taking account of the fact that this will happen. The older you are, therefore, the higher the annuity rate that you can buy will be. For income drawdown to be worthwhile, therefore, you need to get an investment return high enough each year to beat the increase in the annuity rate you could have had that year, *after* taking account of the extra charges you will have to meet. To succeed you may need to be involved in riskier investments than you would like.

A number of providers market income drawdown arrangements now. With some, you are tied into the products (and therefore the investment skills) of one particular provider. With others, called self-invested personal pensions (SIPPs) (see pages 214–215), you have more control and can move between investment funds if you feel you could do better elsewhere.

It is unlikely that annuity rates are going to improve much over the next few years at least, so no one should think of income drawdown as simply a 'temporary parking place' until they can do better from an annuity.

Another motive for many people is that it will mean that they retain the capital in their own possession so that, if they die within a few years, it can go to their family (though with a 35 per cent tax charge). Strong though this motive can be, it is worth checking with your potential heirs about whether they feel the same way; they might prefer to see your capital used to provide greater security in your retirement, rather than preserved to pass to them.

Effects of deferring the purchase of an annuity

	Immediate purchase (age 65)		One year delay (age 66)		Two year delay (age 67)		Three year delay (age 68)	
	50/50 equities/cash pension fund £	Equity pension fund £	50/50 equities/cash pension fund £	Equity pension fund £	50/50 equities/cash pension fund £	Equity pension fund £	50/50 equities/cash pension fund £	Equity pension fund £
Annual annuity rate	7,617	7,617	8,318	8,476	8,935	9,279	9,706	10,272
Income lost on deferral	0	0	7,671	7,671	15,342	15,342	23,013	23,013
Annuity income difference on initial rate of £7,671	0	0	647	805	1,264	1,608	2,035	2,601
Value of pension fund*	100,000	100,000	105,000	107,000	110,250	114,490	115,763	122,504
Years to catch up	0	0	11.9	9.5	12.1	9.5	11.3	8.8

What the table shows: Effects on annuity rates; income lost; fund increase; and time it would take to catch up when deferring purchase of annuity past age 65. Annuity rate figures for a 65-year-old, as at 4 November 2003. * Assuming rises of 7% for equity-based funds and 5% for cash/equity-based funds.

Source: The Annuity Bureau in Money Management, April 2005

Deciding what to buy

The higher that annuity rates are when you make your purchase, the bigger the annuity will be in return for the lump sum you have paid for it. The other side of this, however, is that when interest rates come down (as they have in the last few years), the annuity will be smaller for the same lump sum.

In addition, life expectancy for pensioners – or at least for those who have a reasonable income to live on – is going up. Most of us would view this as a good thing, of course, but it does mean that the same sum of money has to be spread over a longer period. So this too is increasing the cost of future annuities. For example, according to the Annuity Bureau, in June 1995 a 65-year-old couple with a £100,000 pension fund could have bought a joint-life annuity of £9,546 a year, whereas today the same sum of money would buy them only £6,573.

Drawdown, or an alternatively secured pension, only makes sense if looked at as part of overall financial planning, taking all your capital and income into account. Unless you have a substantial fund, you need other sources of income before having an unsecured pension becomes a sensible proposition. Otherwise, you could find that a fall in the market leaves you short of money, at a time when your commitments are not reducing.

Age and state of health matter, as does your own attitude to risk, and to the need to keep a close eye on your investments. Some people enjoy checking their portfolio and understanding the finer points of the tax system, while for others it will only make them anxious. The answers to these questions may change as you get older, or your health or that of your spouse deteriorates.

If you have several pension policies, or one of the policies that is arranged in 'clusters', an alternative to drawdown may be to delay drawing an annuity from some of them to begin with, if you do not need the money straightaway, and so benefit later from increased annuity levels due to your age.

Shopping around

Annuity rates vary considerably between providers, so you could improve your pension by up to 30 per cent by shopping around. However, there will also be a fee or commission to pay to your adviser, so taking up the OMO may not be worthwhile if you have only a small fund. (One adviser puts the breakpoint at around £30,000.) It will almost always be worth enquiring about this, perhaps with one of the specialist independent financial advisers who deals with annuities, even if you do not go ahead.

✱ Action Points

Get independent financial advice and shop around before finalising your annuity purchase.

It is *essential* that you get good advice before going into drawdown, and that you do not enter into any arrangements that you do not understand.

If you take the decision to defer drawing an annuity, or to go for an unsecured pension, review it regularly. The five-yearly review required by law may be too long – every year or two would be better, especially if your health changes.

For more information, see the FSA Factsheet *Your Pension: It's Time to Choose,* which is available free from the FSA at the address on page 262.

FURTHER INFORMATION

This part of the book gives a glossary of pension terms and a list of pension organisations that can be approached for further information about pensions. It also has a list of publications from Age Concern Books, information about obtaining Age Concern England factsheets, and an index to help you find your way around the book.

GLOSSARY

This glossary (with the exception of entries marked *, which are additions or amendments) is taken from the Plain English Campaign's A–Z of Pensions, with their permission. It is available on their website at www.plainenglish.co.uk and you can contact them at PO Box 3, New Mills, High Peak SK22 4QP.

Accrual rate In a defined-benefit scheme this is the rate at which pension benefits build up for the member. They will get a certain amount for each year of pensionable service.

Actuarial valuation* This is an assessment done, usually every three years, by the actuary to work out what money needs to be put into the scheme in the future, to ensure that the pensions can be paid.

Actuary An actuary is an expert on pension scheme assets and liabilities, life expectancy and probabilities (the likelihood of things happening) for insurance purposes. An actuary works out whether enough money is being paid into a pension scheme to pay the pensions when they are due.

Additional Pension* This is what the Government sometimes calls the pension paid by S2P/SERPS.

Additional Voluntary Contribution (AVC) This is an extra amount (contribution) a member can pay to their own pension scheme to increase the future pension benefits.

Alternatively secured pension (ASP)* This is a new arrangement (after April 2006) in which you can draw pension directly from your fund even if you are aged over 75, rather than having to buy an annuity from an insurance company.

Annuity* This is a fixed or increasing amount of money paid each year until a particular event (such as a death). It might be split into more than one payment, for example monthly payments. Many schemes use an annuity to pay pensions. When someone retires, their pension scheme can make a single payment, usually to an insurance company. This company will then pay an annuity to the member. The money paid to the member is what people usually call their pension.

Annuity rate This compares the size of an annuity (how much it pays each year) with how much it cost to buy. It also takes into account the age of the annuitant.

Appropriate personal pension (APP)* This is a personal pension approved for contracting out of S2P/SERPS. Rebate-only (or minimum contributions) APPs are those funded only by rebates of NI contributions and tax relief paid over by HM Revenue & Customs to the pension provider, with no other money going in.

Band earnings* These are your earnings between the Lower and Upper Earnings Limits, used to calculate how much pension you receive from the State Second Pension (and previously SERPS).

Basic Pension This is what the Government sometimes calls the Basic State Pension.

Basic State Pension This is a pension paid by the Government to people who have enough qualifying years. It is not earnings related.

Beneficiaries* These are the people who are paid money, or might be paid in the future, from a pension scheme. For example, they include the individual who is actually paying into the scheme, and also his or her spouse and children who will be paid money if the member should die before they do.

Benefit statement This is a statement of the pension benefits a member has earned. It may also give a prediction of what their final pension might be.

Benefits* With pension schemes, this is everything the member gets after retiring because they were part of the scheme. It usually means the money paid to the member as their pension, as well as their retirement lump sum. It could also include death benefits. With insurance, this is the money the insurance firm pays out if something happens. For example, a life assurance policy would pay death benefits if the insured person dies.

Buy-out policy* This is an insurance policy which pension scheme trustees can buy for a member instead of paying them pension benefits. The insurance company will pay the member (or the member's dependants) a pension, either immediately or when it becomes due.

Career-average scheme* This is a type of occupational pension scheme where the pension is worked out on a formula using your earnings record throughout your working life, revalued to take account of the changes in prices or earnings.

Commutation factor* Most salary-related occupational pension schemes allow you to turn some of your pension into a lump sum at retirement. This is called 'commuting' your pension, and the 'commutation factor' is the price at which you sell your pension back to the scheme. For example, you might get £12 in cash for every £1 you give up.

Contracted out This term is used to describe a scheme where the members contract out of the State Second Pension (S2P).

Contributions This is the money paid into a pension fund for a member. It can be paid by a member or an employer. Contributions are sometimes called pension premiums.

Deferred pension* This is a pension left in a pension scheme, when someone stops being an active or contributing member.

Defined-benefit (DB) scheme This is where the rules of the scheme decide how much pension the member will get. There are different ways of working out the size of the pension, but the member will know which system the scheme uses. The most common type of defined-benefit scheme is a final-salary scheme.

Defined-contribution (DC) scheme This is where the size of the member's pension is not decided by the rules of the scheme. The size of the member's pension will be affected by how much money is put into the pension fund for the member, how much the pension fund has grown, and what annuity rate is available when the member retires. This system is also called a money-purchase scheme.

Earnings cap* This is a limit on how much of a member's earnings is allowed to be used to work out the limits on contributions and benefits in an approved scheme. This limits the amount that a high earner can put into a pension scheme and still get tax relief.

Earnings-related scheme See Salary-related scheme.

Final-salary scheme* This is a type of occupational pension scheme where your pension is worked out on a formula using your earnings from your last year, or the last few years, before retirement.

Free-Standing Additional Voluntary Contributions (FSAVCs)* These are extra contributions that members can pay Into arrangements outside their own pension scheme to increase their pensions.

FRS17* This is the 'financial reporting standard' followed by auditors when they decide what figures to give for the cost of pensions in a company's accounts. For a defined-contribution scheme, it is simply the contributions made. For a defined-benefit scheme, the auditor has to decide whether more or less has been paid into the scheme than was needed at the time, and allow for this in the figures that are used. One effect is that if the company gives the workers better pension benefits, the costs will mean that the company's profits are reduced for that year.

Funding* This means setting aside money now, to pay for pensions in the future. The contributions are invested, so that the future income can be added to the fund and increase what is available.

Graduated Pension scheme This was an additional State pension which was building up before 5 April 1975.

Group Personal Pension (GPP)* This is a system where several employees at one company join a personal pension scheme with the same pension firm. Each member has a separate policy with the pension firm, but contributions are collected together by the employer and passed on.

Guaranteed Minimum Pension (GMP) A member of a contracted-out occupational pension scheme will get at least this much pension unless:

- the member's service is all after 5 April 1997. Their benefits would then come under Limited Price Indexation (LPI);
- some of the member's service is after 5 April 1997. They would have some of their benefits affected by GMP and some by LPI; or
- the scheme is a contracted-out money-purchase scheme. The member's benefits are then affected by Protected Rights.

Home Responsibilities Protection (HRP)* This is the way in which the Department for Work and Pensions (DWP) reduces the number of years in which you have to pay National Insurance contributions in order to get a full pension, if you have spent part of your working life at home looking after children or dependants.

Income drawdown This is when a member retires, but chooses not to buy an annuity straightaway. Until the member buys an annuity, they take an income from the scheme. This is also known as income withdrawal or a drawdown facility.

Lifetime Allowance (LTA)* Under HMRC's new rules from April 2006, this is the maximum pension fund (or capital value of the pension in a DB scheme) that an individual can have tax relief on. It will start at £1.5m in April 2006, and be increased over future years.

Limited Price Indexation (LPI)* This means that the pension is increased each year by either the Retail Prices Index (the measurement of how prices have risen) or 5 per cent, whichever is the lower.

Lower Earnings Limit (LEL)* This is the least amount someone must earn before they start to build up benefits in the National Insurance system.

Migrant member relief* This is a set of tax relief arrangements, under HMRC's new rules from April 2006, for the pensions of people going to work abroad, or coming from abroad to work here.

Minimum Funding Requirement (MFR)* This is a set of rules, laid down by the Government in *The Pensions Act 1995*, for how much money a final-earnings scheme must have in it to pay for the benefits that have been promised. The calculations are done by the actuary, on the basis of a standardised set of assumptions. The MFR has not worked very well, and the Government plans to abolish it.

Money-purchase scheme This is where the size of the member's pension is worked out by the money-purchase method. The size of the member's pension will be affected by how much money is put into the pension fund for the member, how much the pension fund has grown, and what annuity rate is available when the member retires. This is also called a defined-contribution scheme.

National Insurance (NI)* This is money that the Government takes from both workers and employers. The amount depends on how much the worker earns. Some government benefits, such as the Basic State Pension and S2P/SERPS, depend on how much National Insurance you have paid.

Normal Minimum Pension Age (NMPA)* This is the minimum age at which you can take a non-State pension, under HMRC's new rules from April 2006. For most people, it is 50 until April 2010, and 55 after that date, but there are some people who can take their pension earlier than this under the current rules, and their rights are being protected.

Occupational pension* This is a pension scheme set up by an employer or group of employers for their employees.

Open market option (OMO)* This describes the opportunity, when you reach retirement, to shop around for the best-value annuity available from any insurance company, rather than buying one from the company with which you have built up your pension.

Personal pension This is someone's personal pension arrangement. It can also mean a retirement annuity set up before July 1988.

Protected pension ages* Under HMRC's new rules from April 2006, people who have a right to take their pension earlier than the new Normal Minimum Pension Age can retain their protected pension age in the future, subject to certain conditions.

Protected Rights This is the lowest amount of benefits that a contracted-out money-purchase scheme (COMP) can pay to a member. This amount is worked out by using the money-purchase method with the money paid into the scheme as minimum contributions or minimum payments.

Reduced-rate contributions* These are a lower rate of Class 1 NI contributions paid by many married women and widows. They provide no State benefits in the woman's own right, but only as her husband's dependant.

Salary-related scheme This is a scheme where the member's pension depends on their earnings. It is a type of defined-benefit scheme.

Section 32 annuity (also called a Section 32 policy) is another name for a buy-out policy.

Self-invested personal pension (SIPP)* This is a personal pension where the individual chooses where the money should be invested, rather than leaving the decisions to an insurance company. A SIPP is usually only worthwhile if you have a large amount of money in your pension fund.

SERPS *See* State Earnings-Related Pension Scheme.

Small self-administered scheme (SSAS) This is a self-administered occupational pension scheme with no more than 12 members. The scheme will normally be run for a family business. These schemes must meet special conditions, such as having a pensioneer trustee, before they can be approved.

Stakeholder* A stakeholder scheme is a sort of personal pension, which has to meet certain conditions, such as how the scheme is run, and what charges it makes.

State Earnings-Related Pension Scheme (SERPS)* This is the extra State Pension that employed people could earn up to 5 April 2002. They paid extra National Insurance contributions once their earnings reached the Lower Earnings Limit. People could choose to contract out of SERPS by joining an appropriate occupational or personal pension scheme.

State Second Pension (S2P)* This is what the Government replaced the SERPS scheme with in April 2002. It has been designed so that people who do not earn a lot should get a higher pension than they would have had with SERPS.

Substitution contract* This is the contract you have with a new insurance company when you make use of the OMO and buy an annuity from a company different from the one with which you built up your pension.

Superannuation* This is another name for occupational pension. It is now rather an old-fashioned term, but is still used sometimes in the public sector.

Transfer value (TV) This is the amount paid as a transfer payment.

Trustee* This is a person or a company appointed to carry out what the scheme must do. They must follow the laws that apply to trusts.

Unit-linked pension In this type of pension scheme, the benefits depend on what happens to a unitised fund (units in a fund of investments). The scheme is usually linked to the unitised fund through an insurance policy.

Upper Earnings Limit (UEL) This is the highest amount of earnings on which employees pay National Insurance. The employer still pays National Insurance for earnings above this limit.

Waiver of premium benefit* This is an insurance policy you can buy alongside your personal pension scheme, which says that if you can't make your regular payments into the scheme for certain specified reasons such as unemployment or long-term illness, the insurance company will make them instead.

With-profits policy This is a type of insurance policy. It means that a policyholder will get a share of any surplus in the insurance company's life assurance and pensions business.

Working life* This is used to calculate the Basic Pension. It generally lasts from age 16 to just before State Pension age. Currently it is 44 years for a woman and 49 for a man, but it will be 49 years for both sexes when pension ages are equalised in due course.

PENSION ORGANISATIONS

There are many organisations which are involved in pension activity: reporting, marketing or advising. They include those set up under Acts of Parliament, grant-aided organisations, trade bodies, learned societies and certain professional associations. The following is a list of some of these groups and their functions.

Government bodies and semi-official bodies

Department for Work and Pensions (DWP)

This is the government department which is responsible for paying pensions and benefits. It is divided into Jobcentre Plus for people of working age, and The Pension Service, for all pensions and benefits. Look on the website www.thepensionservice.gov.uk for information about which office you should contact, or phone 0845 606 0265 and you will be connected to the pension centre covering your area.

Other useful DWP websites are www.info4pensioners.gov.uk and www.pensionguide.gov.uk

All social security leaflets can be obtained from social security offices or the DWP website (www.dwp.gov.uk), and some can be found in post offices too. Alternatively, you can write to: Pension Guides, Freepost, Bristol BS38 7WA. Tel: 08457 31 32 33.

You can contact **The International Pension Centre** on 0191 218 7777; **The Pension Tracing Service** on 0845 600 2537; and **The State Pension Forecasting Team** on 0845 3000 168 (8am–8pm, Monday to Friday, and 9am–1pm, Saturday. Textphone: 0845 3000 169). The postal address for all these three services is: Tyneview Park, Whitley Road, Benton, Newcastle upon Tyne NE98 1BA. Website: www.thepensionservice.gov.uk

Financial Ombudsman Service (FOS)
South Quay Plaza
183 Marsh Wall
London E14 9SR
Tel: 0845 080 1800
Website: www.financial-ombudsman.org.uk
The FOS helps consumers resolve complaints about most personal finance matters. The service is independent, and free to consumers.

Financial Services Authority (FSA)
25 The North Colonnade
Canary Wharf
London E14 5HS
Consumer helpline: 0845 606 1234
Website: www.fsa.gov.uk/consumer
An independent body set up by the Government to regulate financial services and protect your rights.

Financial Services Compensation Scheme (FSCS)
7th Floor
Lloyds Chambers
Portsoken Street
London E1 8BN
Tel: 020 7892 7300
Website: www.fscs.org.uk

Pays compensation when a financial services company goes out of business.

HM Revenue & Customs

Savings, Pensions and Share Schemes Division

Yorke House

Castle Meadow Road

Nottingham NG2 1BG

Tel: 0115 974 1600

Website: www.hmrc.gov.uk

Grants tax approval for occupational pension schemes and monitors them to ensure that they do not break the rules for tax relief.

National Insurance Contributions Office (NICO)

Benton Park View

Newcastle upon Tyne NE98 1ZZ

Tel: 0845 302 1479

Website: www.hmrc.gov.uk

Deals with National Insurance contribution records and payments. Part of HM Revenue & Customs.

Pension Protection Fund (PPF)

Knollys House

17 Addiscombe Road

Croydon

Surrey CR0 6SR

Tel: 0845 600 2541

Website: www.pensionprotectionfund.org.uk

Pays compensation to members of eligible defined-benefit pension schemes in cases of insolvency.

The Pensions Regulator (tPR)

Napier House

Trafalgar Place

Brighton BN1 4DW

Tel: 0870 606 3636

Website: www.thepensionsregulator.gov.uk

Responsible for regulating occupational pension schemes. Actuaries and auditors have a duty (and anyone else has the power) to 'whistleblow' to the Regulator if they have reasonable cause to believe that the trustees or the employer are breaking the law. Also responsible for registering and supervising stakeholder schemes.

Pensions Advisory Service (TPAS)

11 Belgrave Road

London SW1V 1RB

Tel: 0845 601 2923

Website: www.opas.org.uk

A voluntary organisation which gives advice and information on occupational and personal pensions and helps sort out problems.

Pensions Ombudsman

11 Belgrave Road

London SW1V 1RB

Tel: 020 7834 9144

Website: www.pensions-ombudsman.org.uk

Deals with complaints or disputes about occupational and personal pension schemes. The Ombudsman is appointed by the Government and is independent of the pension providers.

Trade and professional organisations

Association of British Insurers
51 Gresham Street
London EC2V 7HQ
Tel: 020 7600 3333
Website: www.abi.org.uk
Offers advice and information on a wide range of insurance products.

Association of Consulting Actuaries
Warnford Court
29 Throgmorton Street
EC2N 2AT
Tel: 020 7382 4594
Website: www.aca.org.uk
Professional body for actuaries who work as consultants rather than for insurance companies.

Faculty of Actuaries
Maclaurin House
18 Dublin Street
Edinburgh EH1 3PP
Tel: 0131 240 1300
Professional body for actuaries in Scotland.

Institute of Actuaries
Staple Inn Hall
High Holborn
London WC1V 7QJ
Tel: 020 7632 2100
Website: www.actuaries.org.uk
Professional body for actuaries in England and Wales.

Institute of Financial Planning
Whitefriars Centre
Lewins Mead
Bristol BS1 2NT
Tel: 0117 945 2470
Website: www.financialplanning.org.uk
Has a national register of fee-based financial planners.

National Association of Pension Funds (NAPF)
NIOC House
4 Victoria Street
London SW1H 0NX
Tel: 020 7808 1300
Website: www.napf.co.uk
Members are drawn from the larger occupational pension funds and their advisers. NAPF provides an annual survey of statistics relating to pensions and allied topics and advises its members on what it considers good practice.

Pensions Management Institute
4–10 Artillery Lane
London E1 7LS
Tel: 020 7247 1452
Website: www.pensions-pmi.org.uk
Aims to promote high professional standards in the pensions industry; the major examining board for pension qualifications.

Public Concern at Work

Suite 301

16 Baldwin Gardens

London EC1N 7RJ

Tel: 020 7404 6609

Website: www.pcaw.co.uk

Provides free help to prospective whistleblowers.

Society of Pension Consultants

St Bartholomew House

92 Fleet Street

London EC4Y 1DG

Tel: 020 7353 1688

Website: www.spc.uk.com

Consists of financial advisers, actuaries, and pensions and investment management consultants; acts as a lobbying platform for its members.

ABOUT AGE CONCERN

Age Concern is the UK's largest organisation working for and with older people to enable them to make more of life. We are a federation of over 400 independent charities which share the same name, values and standards.

We believe that ageing is a normal part of life, and that later life should be fulfilling, enjoyable and productive. We enable older people by providing services and grants, researching their needs and opinions, influencing government and media, and through other innovative and dynamic projects.

Every day we provide vital services, information and support to thousands of older people of all ages and backgrounds. Age Concern also works with many older people from disadvantaged or marginalised groups, such as those living in rural areas or black and minority ethnic elders.

Age Concern is dependent on donations, covenants and legacies.

Age Concern England
1268 London Road
London SW16 4ER
Tel: 020 8765 7200
Fax: 020 8765 7211
Website:
www.ageconcern.org.uk

Age Concern Scotland
113 Rose Street
Edinburgh EH2 3DT
Tel: 0131 220 3345
Fax: 0131 220 2779
Website:
www.ageconcernscotland.org.uk

Age Concern Cymru
Ty John Pathy
4th Floor
1 Cathedral Road
Cardiff CF11 9SD
Tel: 029 2037 1566
Fax: 029 2239 9562
Website: www.accymru.org.uk

Age Concern Northern Ireland
3 Lower Crescent
Belfast BT7 1NR
Tel: 028 9024 5729
Fax: 028 9023 5497
Website: www.ageconcernni.org.uk

PUBLICATIONS FROM AGE CONCERN BOOKS

Age Concern Books publishes over 65 books, training packs and learning resources aimed at older people, their families, friends and carers, as well as professionals working with and for older people. Publications include:

Your Rights
A guide to money benefits for older people
Sally West

Your Rights has established itself as *the* money benefits guide for older people. Updated annually, and written in clear, jargon-free language, it ensures that older people – and their advisers – can easily understand the complexities of State benefits and discover the full range of financial support available to them.

Updated annually. For details of the current edition, please contact Age Concern Books.

Your Taxes and Savings
A guide for older people
Paul Lewis

This book explains how the tax system affects older people, including how to avoid paying more than necessary. The information about savings and investments covers the wide range of opportunities now available.

Updated annually. For details of the current edition, please contact Age Concern Books.

Using Your Home as Capital

Cecil Hinton and Mark Goodale

Many older people find themselves short of money, yet live in their own, often valuable, properties. Through a wide variety of schemes, people aged 55 and over can now use the value of their homes to obtain a lump sum of capital or a regular additional income, whilst continuing to live at home. This book highlights the benefits – and the problems – which can arise. It gives independent, objective and practical advice.

Updated annually. For details of the current edition, please contact Age Concern Books.

Retiring to Spain

Cyril Holbrook

Once free of the shackles of earning a living, thousands of people make the momentous move to head south to the sun. Living abroad is an entirely different experience from going there on holiday. This book will help you avoid many of the pitfalls, and make the transition to a sunny and healthy retirement a reality. It contains chapters on:

- Pros and cons of living abroad
- Where to settle
- When to move
- Finances
- Property
- Town halls and taxes
- Motoring matters
- Quality of life
- Pets and pastimes
- Healthcare
- Security
- Common complaints
- Going home.

It also contains anecdotes and stories to illustrate the points made, as well as a list of useful contacts and addresses.

£7.99 + p&p   0-86242-385-6

Your Guide to Retirement
Ro Lyon

This bestselling book encourages everyone to view retirement as an opportunity. It is full of useful suggestions and information on:
- managing money: pensions, tax, savings, wills
- making the most of your time: learning and leisure, earning money
- your home: moving, repairing, security, raising income
- staying healthy: looking after yourself, help with health costs
- relationships: sexuality, bereavement, caring for someone.

It is an invaluable guide for people coming up to retirement, planning ahead for retirement, or newly retired, as well as for employers and welfare advisers.

£7.99 + p&p   0-86242-350-3

Everyday Computer Activities
A step by step guide for older home users
Jackie Sherman
£7.99 + p&p   0-86242-403-8

Getting the Most from Your Computer
A practical guide for older home users: 2nd edition
Jackie Sherman
£7.99 + p&p   0-86242-392-9

How to be a Silver Surfer
A beginner's guide to the internet: 2nd edition
Emma Aldridge
£5.99 + p&p   0-86242-379-1

Taking Control: Bladder and Bowel Problems

Kerry Lee

Bladder and bowel problems can affect both men and women, of all ages, and can lead to feelings of anxiety, embarrassment and despair. This excellent guide, complete with relevant case studies, breaks the taboo subject of such problems and provides answers to questions that will enable readers to feel more in control of their problem.

Chapters include:

- Causes of bladder and bowel problems
- Help available
- Dealing with related issues
- Bladder problems
- Bowel problems.

£6.99 + p&p   0-86242-386-4

Taking Control of your Pain

Toni Battison

One in seven people in the UK suffer from chronic pain. Whilst much progress has been made in recent years towards understanding and managing pain, it can still pose a major problem. This book gives essential guidance on how to control pain effectively. It is full of practical information and support, as well as signposting readers to other relevant sources of help and advice.

Chapters include:

- Pain – physical and psychological effects
- Pain – types and common causes
- Diagnosis and assessment
- Dealing with pain – orthodox and self-help treatments
- Stress relief and non-orthodox treatments
- Looking at your lifestyle.

£6.99 + p&p   0-86242-387-2

To order from Age Concern Books

Call our **hotline: 0870 44 22 120** (for orders or a free books catalogue)

Opening hours 9am–7pm Monday to Friday, 9am–5pm Saturday and Sunday

Books can also be ordered from our secure online bookshop: **www.ageconcern.org.uk/shop**

Alternatively, you can write to Age Concern Books, Units 5 and 6 Industrial Estate, Brecon, Powys LD3 8LA. Fax: 0870 8000 100. Please enclose a cheque or money order for the appropriate amount plus p&p made payable to Age Concern England. Credit card orders may be made on the order hotline.

Our **postage and packing** costs are as follows: mainland UK and Northern Ireland: £1.99 for the first book, 75p for each additional book up to a maximum of £7.50. For customers ordering from outside the mainland UK and NI: credit card payment only; please telephone for international postage rates or email sales@ageconcernbooks.co.uk

Bulk order discounts

Age Concern Books is pleased to offer a discount on orders totalling 50 or more copies of the same title. For details, please contact Age Concern Books on 0870 44 22 120.

Customised editions

Age Concern Books is pleased to offer a free 'customisation' service for anyone wishing to purchase 500 or more copies of most titles. This gives you the option to have a unique front cover design featuring your organisation's logo and corporate colours, or adding your logo to the current cover design. You can also insert an additional four pages of text for a small additional fee. Existing clients include many prominent names in British industry, retailing and finance, the trade union movement, educational establishments, public, private and voluntary sectors, and welfare associations. For full details, please contact Sue Henning, Age Concern Books, Astral House, 1268 London Road, London SW16 4ER. Fax: 020 8765 7211. Email: sue.henning@ace.org.uk

Age Concern Information Line/Factsheets subscription

Age Concern produces 50 comprehensive factsheets designed to answer many of the questions older people (or those advising them) may have. These include money and benefits, health, community care, leisure and education, and housing. For up to five free factsheets, telephone 0800 00 99 66 (8am–7pm, seven days a week, every week of the year). Alternatively you may prefer to write to Age Concern, FREEPOST (SWB 30375), ASHBURTON, Devon TQ13 7ZZ.

For professionals working with older people, the factsheets are available on an annual subscription service, which includes updates throughout the year. For further details and costs of the subscription, please contact Age Concern at the above Freepost address.

We hope that this publication has been useful to you. If so, we would very much like to hear from you. Alternatively, if you feel that we could add or change anything, then please write and tell us, using the following Freepost address: Age Concern, FREEPOST CN1794, London SW16 4BR.

INDEX

See also Glossary (pp. 252–61)

A

'A-Day' 123

'abatement' rules 34, 187, 188

abroad, living *see* expatriates

accrual rates 97, 139

'actuarial reductions' 182, 183

actuaries 172, 173

Additional Pension 55–56, 62, 66, 75, 112

  see also SERPS; State Second Pension

Additional Voluntary Contributions (AVCs) 28, 33, 98, 115, 121, 161, 162–63, 165, 166, 167

  and early retirement 184

adoption leave 50, 153

advice, getting *see* financial advisers; Pensions Advisory Service

age discrimination 188

age-related additions 61

alternatively secured pensions 127, 128, 214, 245, 248

annual allowances (of 'pension input') 124–25

annuities, buying in appropriate personal pensions 113

  in cash-balance schemes 97–98

  in COMPs 112

  compulsory purchase 240–41, 244

  cost of 243

  in DC schemes 127–28

  deferring 169, 247

  'impaired life' 33, 239, 240

  investment-linked 239, 241–42

  joint-life 243, 248

  non-investment-linked 238, 239

  personal pension 237–43, 246, 247, 248–49

  purchased life 241, 244

  'relevant' 128, 245

  short-term 127, 128

  tax restrictions on 243–44

  unit-linked 239, 241–42

  value-protected 243

  with profits 239, 242

  with proportion 243

APPs *see* appropriate personal pensions

Attendance Allowance 50, 57

AVCs *see* Additional Voluntary Contributions

B

band earnings 56

Basic Pension *see under* State Pensions

benefits and allowances, State 23–24, 27, 34, 35

  Attendance Allowance 50, 57

  Carer's Allowance 49, 50, 57

  Child Benefit 49, 51

  disability benefits 50, 57, 83, 84, *see also* Incapacity Benefit

Jobseeker's Allowance 48, 50, 53, 86–88, 89
means-tested see Council Tax Benefit; Housing Benefit; Pension Credit
and same-sex couples 39–40
and sex change 40–41
and State Pensions 77–78
and unmarried couples 40
for widows/widowers 65–66, 70, 110
Bereavement Allowance 65–66, 70, 110
Bereavement Payments 65
broken employment records 12, 27, 31, 74–75, 227–29
'buy-out' bonds see Section 32 'buy-out' bonds
buy-to-let housing 24

C

Capita (company) 102, 104
career-average salary schemes 92, 95–97, 115, 140
carers
and Home Responsibilities Protection 49–51
and State Second Pensions 57
Carer's Allowance 49, 50, 57
cash-balance schemes 92, 97–98, 115, 140
Child Benefit 49, 51
Child Tax Credit 66, 84
CIMP see contracted-in money purchase schemes
Civil Partnerships 39–40, 70, 110, 157

Civil Service pension scheme 95–96, 100, 102, 159
closed pension schemes 190–92
and consultation 192–93
coal industry 103
Combined Pension Forecasts 20, 62
COMP see contracted-out money-purchase schemes
company pension schemes see occupational pension schemes
compensation schemes 107, 226
complaints, making 30, 199–200, 226–27, 229
consultation regulations 165, 192–93, 195
contract-based pensions 91, 101, 106–107
contracted-in money-purchase (CIMP) schemes 112
contracted-out money-purchase (COMP) schemes 107, 108, 111–12, 118, 120, 147
leaving 175
and lump sums 141, 144
Protected Rights fund 112–13, 141
spouses' pensions 113, 157
women 149
and working after retirement age 187
contracted-out salary-related (COSR) schemes 107, 108–11, 186
'cooling off' periods 225

COSR *see* contracted-out salary-related schemes
Council Tax Benefit 23, 77–78, 80, 81–82, 87
credits *see under* National Insurance contributions
'crystallisation' 125–26, 169

D

DB schemes *see* defined-benefit schemes
DC schemes *see* defined-contribution schemes
death benefits 126, 130–31, 138, 154–58
'decision trees' 221
deferred pensions
  occupational 168, 169, 170–71, 175, 186–87, 188
  personal 231, 247
  State 38–39, 42, 73, 75–79
Deficiency Notices 31, 55, 74–75
defined-benefit schemes 91, 92, 93–98, 105, 107, 114, 115, 118, 138, 139–40, 146
  accrual rates 139
  annual allowances 124
  career-average salary 92, 95–97, 115, 140
  cash-balance 92, 97–98, 115, 140
  and change of employer 179
  contracted-out 107, 108–11, 117–20
  contributions to 142
  deferred pensions 170–71, 175

final-salary 92, 93–95, 99, 102, 115, 139–40
  HMRC top limits 138
  lump sums 34, 140–42
  and 'pensionable service' 139, 140
  refunds on leaving 168
  statutory 102
  transfer values 172, 173, 175, 176
  trust-based 104, 105
defined-contribution (money-purchase) schemes 34, 91, 92, 98–100, 105, 106–107, 107, 114, 115, 117, 138, 143–45, 147
  after April 2006 127–28
  annual allowances 124
  buying extra 167
  and change of employer 179, 181
  contract-based 106–107
  contracted-out 107, 108, 143
  contributions to 143, 144
  and death benefits 157
  and early retirement 183–84
  HMRC top limits 138
  and ill health 183–84
  'income protection' 183
  to join or not to join? 147
  'permanent health insurance' 184
  preserved ('paid-up') pensions 175
  statutory 102
  taking transfers 175, 176

trust-based 104, 105
winding up 196
and women 149
and working after retirement age
187
Department for Work and
Pensions (DWP) 14, 68, 220
dependants
and State Pensions 42–43
see also widows/widowers
deposit-based personal policies
207, 209
Disability and Sickness Allowance
83
disability benefits 50, 57, 84
see also Incapacity Benefit
Disability Living Allowance 50, 84
disputes 199–200
divorced people 10, 12, 32, 40,
70–71, 158–60, 230
and pension sharing 71,
158–60, 230
DWP see Department for Work
and Pensions

E

early retirement 32, 33, 82,
181–84
ill-health 33, 83–86, 182,
183–84, 185–86, 204, 211
and Jobseeker's Allowance
86–88
and personal pensions 184,
234–35
and protected pension ages
135
and protecting State Pension 89

'earnings cap', pensionable 121
earnings-related schemes see
contracted-out salary-related
schemes
Earnings Threshold (ET) 46–47, 54
electricity industry 103–104
employment, changing 168–81
Employment Tribunals 151, 200
Equitable Life 208
ET see Earnings Threshold
expatriates 32, 35, 64
and Incapacity Benefit 84
and 'migrant member tax relief'
131–32
'expression of wish' forms 27,
154

F

'fact-finds' 222
family leave 152–53
'final pensionable earnings'
139–40, 160
final-salary schemes 92, 93–95,
107, 115, 139–40
and early retirement 183
when wound up 194–95
financial advisers 28
charges 222–23, 224, 225, 226
and compensation for mis-
selling 107, 226
and 'fact-finds' 222
independent 223, 224, 225,
238
'keyfacts' documents 224
making complaints about
226–27
'tied' 223

Financial Assistance Schemes 198
Financial Ombudsman Service
225, 227
Financial Services Authority (FSA)
14, 119, 176, 213, 219
factsheets and publications
14–15, 220, 221, 227
pension calculators 206
register of financial advisers
224–25
tables of charges 15, 212
Financial Services Compensation
Scheme 107
forecasts, pension 20–21, 61–63,
89, 205, 206
foster parents 50
Free-Standing Additional Voluntary
Contributions (FSAVCs) 28,
101, 106, 121, 161, 164, 165,
166, 167
FSA see Financial Services
Authority
FSAVC see Free-Standing
Additional Voluntary
Contributions
'funeral benefits' 23, 155

G

Gender Recognition Act 2004 40
GMP see Guaranteed Minimum
Pension
GPPs see Group Personal
Pensions
Graduated Pension 38, 60, 62, 75
Group Personal Pensions (GPPs)
101, 106, 138, 212–13, 218,
221, 222

Guaranteed Minimum Pension
(GMP) 109–10, 141, 169, 170,
186
and early retirement 182
guarantees, five-year 156
Guidance Note (GN11) 172

H

HM Revenue & Customs (HMRC;
formerly Inland Revenue) 123
annual allowances 124–25
and crystallisation 125–26
Deficiency Notices 31, 74–75
Lifetime Allowances (LTA)
123–24, 125, 127, 134, 136
pension rules 120–22 (until April
2006), 123–33 (after April
2006)
registration of schemes 123,
133
restrictions on pensions 101,
121, 243–44
tax relief 91, 120–21, 125, 129,
131–32, 206, 210–11
transitional rules 101–102, 121,
124, 133–34
Home Responsibilities Protection
(HRP) 49–51, 52, 53, 54, 75
House of Fraser 98
houses see property
Housing Benefit (HB) 23, 77–78,
80, 81–82, 87
HRP see Home Responsibilities
Protection

I

ill-health, retirement due to 33,
83–86, 182, 183–84, 185–86,
204, 211
and income protection policies
183–84, 211
ill-health pensions 127, 128
Incapacity Benefit 43, 53, 57,
84–85, 89
National Insurance contribution
requirements 85
and occupational and personal
pensions 86
income drawdown/withdrawal
127, 232, 242, 245–46, 248
Income Support 50, 57, 70, 82
bereavement premium 70
increasing pensions
occupational 121, 160–67
personal/stakeholder 164,
235–36
State 74–75
see also deferred pensions
Independent Trustees 196
industrial accidents/disease 66
inflation-proofing 94, 111, 146,
161, 169
information, getting 117, 140,
201–202
Inheritance Tax 131, 154
Inland Revenue see HM Revenue
& Customs
insolvent companies 196–98
insurance companies 114, 120,
164, 169, 172, 196–97, 232
'integrated' schemes 139, 151–52

International Pension Centre 63
Invalid Care Allowance see Carer's
Allowance
investment-linked annuities 239,
241–42
investments 24, 133

J

Jobcentre Plus offices 88
Jobseeker's Allowance 48, 50, 53,
86–88, 89

L

LEL see Lower Earnings Limit
'letters of wishes' 154
LGPS see Local Government
Pension Scheme
'liberation', pension 177–78
life-assurance benefit 154–55
life-assurance premiums, tax relief
on 210–11
life expectancies 9–10
life insurance policies 23
'lifestyle'/'lifecycle' funds 98–99,
217
Lifetime Allowances (LTAs) 27,
123–24, 125–27, 129, 136
and protected pension ages 135
and transitional protection
133–34
loans to employers 132–33
Local Government Pension
Scheme 102–103, 141, 174,
179, 187, 188
low-paid workers 31, 32, 148
see also part-time workers;
women

Lower Earnings Limit (LEL) 45,
46–47, 54, 55, 85
LTAs *see* Lifetime Allowances
lump sums
death benefits 126, 130, 131,
154–55
defined-benefit schemes
140–42
defined-contribution schemes
99, 144
five-year guarantees 156
inherited by spouses 77
occupational pensions 121,
126, 128–30, 140–42
pension protection 156
personal pensions 122, 206,
236–37
from Social Fund 80
State Pensions 39, 76, 78
when terminally ill 129, 186

M
married couples 23, 29, 34, 41
married women
deferred State pensions 42, 76
and Home Responsibilities
Protection 49
reduced-rate contributions
41–42, 51–53, 71
self-employed 48
and separation 72
State Pensions 12, 41–43, 44,
73
see also divorced people;
remarriage
maternity leave 152, 153
'migrant member relief' 131–32

Minimum Funding Requirement
190
minimum pension age 127
mis-selling 176, 226
'money-purchase' schemes *see*
contracted-in, contracted-out
and defined-contribution
schemes
mortality subsidies 242

N
National Health Service scheme
95, 100, 102, 141, 146, 188
National Insurance contributions
11, 37
and Basic Pensions 41, 43–46
classes 46–48
credits 11, 48–49, 53, 89
of deceased people 65
and early retirement 82, 89
employers' 47
and gaps in records 12, 27, 31,
74–75, 228
and Home Responsibilities
Protection 49–51
married women's reduced-rate
41–42, 51–53, 71
rebates 108, 111–12, 113
self-employed people 43, 48
voluntary 48, 52, 53, 54, 63,
74–75, 89
when working abroad 63
National Insurance Fund 111
National Minimum Wage 53
nationalised industries 103, 161
Nationwide 95
'net relevant earnings' 122

NMPA *see* 'normal minimum pension age'
'non-contributory' schemes 142, 165
'normal minimum pension age' (NMPA) 127

O

occupational pensions 13, 114, 28, 107, 137–38, 146–48
buying extra 121, 160–67
closed 190–93
'commuting' (into lump sum) 121
deferred 168, 169, 170–71, 175, 186–87, 188
and divorce 158–60
earmarking 158
employers' changes to 29, 30, 193–94
getting information on 201–202
and Incapacity Benefit 86
and insolvent employers 169, 190
and Jobseeker's Allowance 87
leaving 168–69, *see* transferring
and life insurance policies 23
and personal/stakeholder pensions 122, 164, 232–33
protected pension ages 135
refunds 129, 168
and security 189–90
statutory 100, 101
and tax relief 120, 121, 123
transferring 169, 173–81, 191
trust-based 98, 101, 104–106
women 149–51

and working after retirement age 186–87
wound up 30, 129–30, 194–96
see also defined-benefit schemes
Ombudsman, Pensions 173, 185, 189, 199, 200, 226
see also Financial Ombudsman Service
'open market options' (OMOs) 127, 128, 144, 237, 238, 249
Opra 200
see Regulator, Pensions
Over-80s Pensions 61
overlapping benefits rule 42

P

parental leave 153
part-time workers 31, 32, 54–55, 150, 151–52
paternity leave 153
penalties 132
pension calculators 26, 206
Pension Credit 23–24, 38, 77–78, 79–81
guarantee credit 80, 82
for same-sex couples 40
savings credit 80
and State Pensions 77–78
for umarried couples 40
Pension Protection Fund (PPF) 103, 110, 169, 173, 190, 196, 197–98, 199, 201
Pension Service, The 14, 73, 81
pension sharing 71, 158–60, 230
Pension Tracing Service 60
'pensionable service' 139, 140

pensions
  alternatives to 24–25
  forecasting 20–21, 61–63, 89,
    205, 206
  what sort is yours? 114–17
  see occupational pensions;
    personal pensions;
    stakeholder pensions; State
    pensions
Pensions Act 1995 190
Pensions Act 2004 104, 179,
  181, 192, 193, 197
Pensions Advisory Service (TPAS)
  117, 173, 189, 195, 199–200,
  220
Pensions Commission 9
Pensions Regulator 105, 200–201
Permanent Health Insurance
  payments 86
'Personal Capability Assessment'
  84
personal pensions 13–14, 28, 98,
  114, 203
  appropriate 107, 112, 113–14,
    117, 119, 120, 236–37
  and broken employment
    records 227–29
  Buyer's Guides 233–34
  charges 211–12
  choosing 210, 220–21, 229
    'clusters' of policies 232, 249
  compensation schemes 107
  complaints about 226–27, 229
  contract-based 101, 106–107
    and contracting out of S2P
    118–19
  converting to self-invested
    personal pensions 214–15
  deferring 231, 247
  deposit-based policies 207, 209
  and divorce 230
  and early retirement 184,
    234–35
  estimates of 205, 206
  'Group' (GPPs) 101, 106, 138,
    212–13, 218, 221, 222
  and ill-health 211
  and Incapacity Benefit 86
  increasing 235–36
  and Jobseeker's Allowance 87
  'lifestyle' arrangements 209–10
  limits on contributions 101
  lump sums 236–37
  protected pension ages 135
  regular or single premiums? 212
  self-investment personal
    pensions (SIPPs) 214–15,
    246
  single-premium 176, 212, 228
  starting 206–207
  stopping paying into 230, 231,
    232–34
  suspending contributions 233
  switching investments 209–10
  tax rules 122, 123
  transferring into 174
  and unemployment 234–35
  unit-linked policies 208, 209
  unsecured 34, 35, 245–46
  and waivers of premium benefits
    211, 230, 234, 235
  and widows/widowers 210–11

with-profits policies 207–208, 209

and women 12, 119, 229–30

and working after retirement age 231–32

see also contract-based pensions; defined-contribution schemes

PPF *see* Pension Protection Fund

pregnancy 152, 230

preserved ('paid-up') pensions 170–71, 175

'private' pensions *see* personal pensions; stakeholder pensions

property 21, 24, 160, 133, 214–15

protected pension age 27, 33, 135

Protected Rights 112, 113, 119, 141, 210, 236–37

public sector

'abatement' rules 34, 187, 188

consultations about changes/closures 192

and contracting out of services 178

and early retirement 183

index-linking 170

lump sums 140, 141

statutory schemes 102–104, 111

superannuation 137

'transfer clubs' 169, 173–74, 176

trust-based schemes 104

Q

'qualifying years' 44–46, 54

R

railways schemes 103, 179

'reckonable earnings' 56

Redundancy Fund 198

redundancy pay 88–89, 184, 234, 235

registration of schemes 123, 133

Regulator, Pensions 177, 181, 189, 192, 196, 199, 200–201, 219, 220

Rehabilitation Support Allowance 83

remarriage 52, 66, 71–72

retirement

income needed 10–12, 18–20, 22–23, 26

see also early retirement

retirement age 13, 188

working after 34, 186–88, 231–32

'retirement annuities' 205

S

Sainsbury's 95

'salary sacrifices' 164–65

same-sex couples 29, 39–40, 110

'scheme rescues' 197

Section 32 'buy-out' bonds 168, 169, 174

Section 226 policies 205, 216, 237

self-employed people 114

National Insurance contributions 43, 48

'net relevant earnings' 122
Section 226 policies 216, 237
tax relief 125
self-invested personal pensions
(SIPPs) 28, 214–15, 246
'self-investment' 145
separated couples 72
SERPS (State Earnings-Related
Pension Scheme) 38, 55, 56,
57–58, 59
and Guaranteed Minimum
Pension 170
'Inherited' 67–68, 77
see State Second Pensions
severance payments 184, 234,
235
Severe Disablement Allowance 57
sex changes: and benefits 40–41
short-term annuities 127, 128
SIPPs see self-invested personal
pensions
small self-administered schemes
(SSASs) 28, 145–46, 177–78
Social Fund: lump-sum payments
80
Social Security Appeal Tribunals
85
SSASs see small self-
administered schemes
SSP see Statutory Sick Pay
stakeholder pensions 13–14, 28,
78, 101, 106, 114, 160, 203,
204, 216–17
access via employers 218–19
advantages 166–67
advice on 220–21

buying 220–21
complaints about 226–27
contract-based 101
and contracting out of S2P 118,
119
contribution limits 101, 122, 164
'default funds' 217
and early retirement 184
and financial advisers'
commission 223
Group schemes 101
'lifestyle' arrangements 210,
217, 218
regulation of 219
starting and stopping payments
228, 233
tax rules 122, 123
transferring into 174
trust-based 106, 219
and women 12, 229
and working after retirement age
231–32
State Pensions 10, 11, 34, 37
Additional 55–56, 62, 66, 75,
112
age of drawing 13, 38, 39
age-related additions 61
Basic 38, 41, 43–46, 50, 54,
55, 62
claiming 72–73
deferring 38–39, 42, 73, 75–79
dependent husbands' and
wives' increases 42–43
and divorced people 70–71
and early retirement 89
for expatriates 35, 64

forecasts 20–21, 61–63, 89
Graduated Pension 38, 60, 62, 67, 70, 75
increasing 74–75, *see also* deferring
lump sums 39, 76, 78
'non-contributory' 38
Over-80s 61
payment of 73–74
for same-sex couples 40
for separated people 72
and sex change 40
and tax 77–78
when working after State Pension age 89–90
for widows/widowers 12, 44, 62, 67, 69–70, 76–77
for women 12–13, 29, 38, 39, 41–42
see also State Second Pensions (S2Ps)
State Second Pensions (S2Ps) 38, 48, 53, 56–57, 147
calculating 57–59
contracted in 27, 59, 91, 107, 113–14, 120
contracted out of 27, 59–60, 107, 108-11, 113, 114, 116, 117–20, 204–205, 226, 230, 231
credits 57
and employers' NI contributions 47
'Inherited' 67, 69
and low-paid and part-time workers 55
for women 119
'Statutory Money Purchase Illustrations' 205
statutory pension schemes 91, 100, 101, 102–104, 111
Statutory Sick Pay (SSP) 83, 84
S2Ps *see* State Second Pensions
'superannuation' 105, 137

T

takeovers, company 178–81
tax/tax relief *see* HM Revenue & Customs
teachers' pension schemes 102, 103, 105, 146, 169, 174, 179
terminal illness 186
Tesco 95
TPAS *see* Pensions Advisory Service
trade unions/Trades Union Congress(TUC) 180, 206, 219
Transfer of Undertakings (Protection of Employment) Regulations (TUPE) 178–79
transfers out of occupational pensions 30, 168–69
'bulk' 180
and change of employer 174, 178–81
and closed pension schemes 191
and company reorganisation 181
from defined-benefit to defined-contribution schemes 175–76, 191
'mis-sold' 176

and pension 'liberation' scams
177–78
into personal/stakeholder
pensions 174, 175–76
public sector 173–74, 176
'transfer value analyses' 176
trust-based pension schemes 91,
101, 103, 104–106, 219
trustees 101, 104, 105, 219
and changes or closure
192–94
Independent 196
winding-up schemes 194–96
TUC see trade unions
TUPE see Transfer of
Undertakings
(Protection of Employment)
Regulations

U

UEL see Upper Earnings Limit
unauthorised payments 132
unemployment
and personal pensions 234–35
see Jobseeker's Allowance
unit-linked annuities 239, 241–42
unit-linked personal policies 208,
209
Universities Superannuation
Scheme 105
unmarried couples 12, 29, 110
and benefits 40, 157–58
unsecured pensions 34, 35, 127,
129, 131, 245–46
Upper Earnings Limit (UEL) 46–47

V

'value shifting' 132
voluntary contributions
National Insurance 27, 48, 52,
53, 54, 63, 74–75, 89
see also Additional Voluntary
Contributions; Free-Standing
Additional Voluntary
Contributions

W

waiver of premium benefit 211,
230, 234, 235
Widowed Mother's Allowance
66–67, 69
Widowed Parent's Allowance 66,
69, 110
widows/widowers 10
Bereavement Allowance 65–66
Bereavement Payments 65
and COMP schemes 113
and COSR schemes 110
with dependent children 66–67,
69
Guaranteed Minimum Pensions
110
and Home Responsibilities
Protection 49
inherited SERPS 23, 56, 67–68
inherited State Pensions 76–77
inherited S2P 23, 56, 69
and occupational pensions 156,
157
and personal pensions 210–11
reduced-rate NI contributions
51–53

State Pensions 12, 44, 62, 67, 69–70, *see also* inherited SERPS, State Pensions, S2P
transitional help 70
winding up occupational pension schemes 30, 129–30, 194–96
with-profits annuities 239, 242
with-profits personal policies 207–208, 209
women
  adoption leave 153
  annuity rates 237
  contracting out of S2P 119, 230, 231
  in defined-contribution schemes 149
  maternity leave 152, 153
  and occupational pensions 149–51
  personal/stakeholder pensions 119, 229–30, 231, 237
  State Pensions 12–13, 29, 38, 39, 41–42
  see also divorced couples; married couples; married women; widows/widowers
Work Focused Interviews 83
working after retirement age 34, 186–88
  and age discrimination rules 188
  and personal/stakeholder pensions 231–32
'working life' 44, 45
Working Tax Credit 49, 87